The Peaceful Mind Bible

For

Busy Moms

100 TREASURES OF WISDOM FOR MOMS TO CREATE INNER PEACE

Danielle Thienel

Table of Contents

Are you a mom feeling overwhelmed and struggling to find peace and balance in your life? You're not alone. Juggling the demands of motherhood, work, and everything in between can be a daunting task, leaving many moms feeling depleted and burnt out. That's where "The Peaceful Mind Bible for Busy Moms" comes in. This book is a source of inspiration and teaching for faith-filled moms who are seeking a way to find peace and balance in their busy lives. It offers practical advice, relatable stories, and spiritual guidance to help moms embrace the joy of motherhood and find peace in their daily lives. Whether you're a new mom or a seasoned pro, "The Peaceful Mind Bible for Busy Moms" is the perfect resource to help you navigate the ups and downs of motherhood with grace and peace.

Get ready to discover a treasure trove of wisdom in "The Peaceful Mind Bible"! Inspired by the first 100 episodes of my popular podcast, "The Peaceful Mind Podcast for Busy Moms," this book is jam-packed with tips and strategies to help you find more peace, joy, and balance in your life. As a busy mom myself, I know firsthand how challenging it can be to juggle all the demands of motherhood while still finding time for self-care and personal growth. That's why I created this book - to make the life-changing advice shared on my podcast accessible to even more moms in need. So if you're ready to transform your life and find more peace, joy, and balance in your daily routine, then "The Peaceful Mind Bible" is the perfect resource for you!

I invite you to dive into the pages here reading one topic a day, or several pages in some stolen moments of solitude. If you're struggling with a particular challenge related to your emotional well-being, mindset, personal growth, productivity, or organization, fear not!

Simply scan over the topics and choose one that speaks to you in that moment. Each chapter is designed to offer an injection of peace of mind, wherever and whenever you need it most.

It is vitally important that you make peace a priority in your busy mom life so you can be the calm confident mom God created you to be. When you do, you become an example of what it is to live a happy, healthy, and holy life, which then overflows to your children and family. As a faith-filled Catholic mom and certified life coach, I know full well that we aren't meant to go about this journey alone or at the expense of our own well-being and I hope you will find the inspiration you need in the following pages to turn your moments of overwhelm into a peaceful mom life.

In the name of the Father, and of the Son and of the Holy Spirit, let's get started

xo,
Danielle

                                    DANIELLE THIENEL

Have no anxiety at all, but in everything,
by prayer and petition, with thanksgiving,
make your requests known to God then
the peace of God that surpasses all
understanding will guard your hearts and
minds in Christ Jesus.

-Philippians 4:7

1

It's Never Better Than It Is Right Here

When I was first introduced to this concept, it blew my mind. In fact, I fought against it. Of course, I want things to be better. That's what I'm striving for! But I have to let you know, it really is never better than it is right here.

We've been duped into believing the idea that life will be better once you've achieved X, Y, or Z.

Life will be better when I graduate when I get a better job, when I get married when I have a certain amount of money in the bank, and on and on.

For me, once it was, "life will be better when my kids start putting the cap back on the toothpaste." That was a real thing that put me over the edge sometimes! But life doesn't work like that.

Once my kids started putting the cap back on the toothpaste, the peace was fleeting. It lasted for a day because then I saw the lights left on, the clothes on the floor, and empty cereal bowls everywhere.

The true secret is that it's never our outside circumstances that cause the feelings we seek. It is always our thoughts. You will still have the same human brain when you get to that place where you think everything will be better. You'll still get to choose what you believe and still be challenged by the highs and lows of life.

Feeling proud, successful, joyful, or peaceful is all at your fingertips right now. You should still have big dreams and aspire to great things, but hurrying to a new place is unnecessary.

You can have peace of mind right here.

2

Four Steps For More Peace

Creating more peace in your life isn't as hard as you might think. My story is a testament to how making peace a priority can profoundly shift every aspect of your life. This shift comes from your decision to put your quest for more peace at the front and center of your life.

If you're ready to ditch the stress and overwhelm for more peace, here are four steps you can take right now to get relief.

Step One: Determine your why

Why are you ready to seek more peace? Like any project we undertake, we need to have a sustaining reason for why we want to accomplish this.

Dig in and search for your why. Make sure it's big and powerful enough to keep you moving forward on your journey.

Step Two: Gather courage

It's not uncommon to weigh the risks, take stock of all ahead, and feel fearful of what we perceive to be a hard journey. But instead of derailing yourself before you even begin, gather courage by focusing on those things that help you feel strong.

I suggest this focus be your faith. With faith, fear cannot remain intact. Take courage along the journey to making peace a priority in your motherhood.

Step Three: Commit and Recommit

No matter how many times you've tried and failed, keep committing and recommitting. You owe it to yourself not to give up!

If you keep going, you can't fail. Failure only happens when you stop trying.

Step Four: Carve our dedicated, daily time to spend with God

It can be five minutes of silent prayer as you nurse your newborn. It can be talking with God out loud while you do your thing around the house. Maybe it looks like journaling to Him while you wait in the school pick-up line or listening to the audio version of the Bible while you're on a walk.

There are many different ways to make time for Him in our lives. As you do, He promises to strengthen your faith, deepen your friendship, build trust, give guidance and clarity, and ultimately grant you the gift of His peace.

3

How To Generate Confidence In Yourself

When we are confident we are more likely to move forward and go after what we truly want. We are more likely to seize opportunities instead of backing away from them. And, if things don't work out at first, being confident in our abilities helps us try again.

There are two steps you can take to generate more confidence in yourself.

First, become a person who is consistently following through on your word to yourself.

You can't just sit around and wait for confidence to show up before you follow through on your commitments; it doesn't work that way. It comes after you practice following through on your commitments to yourself.

Next, take courage.

The answer to procrastination is courage. Having courage doesn't mean you won't feel fear, but it means that even through the fear, you'll take action anyway.

With these two steps, you'll see that you are, in fact, capable of doing hard, scary, vulnerable, embarrassing, adventurous, and seemingly impossible things.

With more self-confidence, you'll set more goals, take more risks, talk to more people, and take more action in your life. You'll build beliefs around your capability. And this will allow you to dream and live into a bigger future. Failure is no longer the worst thing that can happen to you.

You'll be fully alive in the adventurous and peaceful life God created for you.

Peace In Parenting

As parents, we all make mistakes and missteps and do things we wish we wouldn't have. But I want you to become aware of the story you are telling yourself about your parenting.

Are you telling yourself things that serve you and bring you peace? If not, I want you to consider the option that you have to let go of what you don't like about your past parenting endeavors.

Forgive and forget the mistakes you think you made as a parent. Stop bringing yourself suffering over things that can't be changed. Those things were supposed to happen because they DID happen.

Work at re-writing the story of your past parenting in a way that brings you feelings of peace instead of regret. The past is over. It can't be changed. Wanting things to be different only brings you pain now.

You can rewrite the story by looking at everything you did right. Keep all the good parts, like how you made every doctor's visit, threw them the best birthday parties, or watched and prayed over them while they slept.

Remember those chapters. Tell the story of how you did your best with what you had at the time. Remind yourself that your intentions were always good. Your heart desires to be the best parent you can be with your human frailties and misgivings. You continue to learn and try again.

You have so much more that did go right than wrong. Choose to concentrate on that and have peace in your parenting.

5

When you find yourself in a busy season of life, it can be hard to find peace. Maybe you feel this way around the holidays, at the end of the school year, or in the craziness of the summer.

Whenever this lack of peace presents itself, I'd like to offer three strategies to help minimize the stress and prepare your heart for more peace.

1 - Minimize distractions

There is so much vying for our attention, so many things that pull us away from what would give us a peaceful heart. Are any of the following taking up too much of your time right now: social media, email checking, watching the news, or one more episode of something on Netflix?

These things are not bad; I'm not saying you shouldn't do them. However, when you are saying yes to one of those things, you are saying no to something else that may be of more importance. Peace of mind and heart naturally happen when you focus, commit, and follow through with what matters most to you.

Start today to put away distractions that don't align with your priorities.

2 - Focus on aligning your thoughts and life with Christ

Our faith tells us that God has a plan. There is His will, and He makes good of everything. He is a positive thinker, so we, too, can think positively about our past and what is happening right now.

Are you God-minded about your current circumstances? What do you think about yourself?

God-minded thinking would believe that you are worthy and loved. It would believe there is no need to hurry; all will get done. It is praising the Lord despite any problems you may be facing.

Prepare your heart for peace by talking to Him and listening to His response. It will come in the way of peace.

3 - Ask yourself, "How can I give love today?"

When you ask yourself powerful questions like this one, your mind will go to work on your behalf to search and find powerful and useful answers. When you can think loving thoughts, send out loving prayers, and carry out acts of love, it shifts your life immensely.

As a mom, I know how much you are already doing for everyone, but sometimes it gets to a point where our doings have an energy of obligation, exhaustion, or even a touch of resentment. Asking this purposeful question can help dispel any negative emotions and guard your heart by guarding your mind first.

A Formula For Peace

1 - Put prayer into practice

Prayer doesn't have to be complicated. Prayer can simply be a focused thought toward heaven. But regardless of how you pray, to have and sustain peace, you must build some sort of prayer practice.

I invite you to consider this an easy step, not a daunting task. Just ask yourself where you could put prayer into your life right now. However it looks for you, a prayer practice will help you move toward sustaining peace in your life.

2 - Patient perseverance

Patience is necessary for peace, but it's not the ability to wait that matters. Waiting is inevitable in this life. Patience is learning how to keep a good attitude while waiting. That should be the focus.

We need to learn to enjoy where we are on the way to where we are going because, in this life, we won't get everything immediately. If you focus on your attitude along the way, patience will naturally follow.

3 - Progress, not perfection

I'm a recovering perfectionist. Now instead, I focus on making progress toward what I want out of life instead of needing things to be perfect before I do anything.

                                   DANIELLE THIENEL

There is no such thing as perfect until we get to heaven. Therefore trying to look, feel, behave, or believe you need to be perfect is a false objective before doing something. The reality is nothing will ever be perfect, but focusing on progress, not perfection, will allow you to reach your goals while maintaining your peace.

7

1 - Pray every day

It doesn't have to be long. It doesn't have to be structured. It just needs to be every day. Prayer is what you need to connect and be filled up. I have found it makes my life easier and smoother because when I take time to connect with Christ, he shows me the way.

2 - Drop perfectionism

Make it your mission to recognize when you feel as if you have to be perfect. Then, instead of focusing on perfection, draw a line and decide you just have to put out B- work. That way, you can get unstuck from the trap of perfectionism and make progress on what matters.

3 - Forgive yourself

It's constant work to get to the place in our life where we want to be. Instead of spending your time beating yourself up about your mistakes, use that energy to practice forgiving yourself.

4 - Love where you are

You can love the present. Look for what's good in what's happening. That is where your power lies. You don't have to fight with reality. Your thoughts are in your control right now!

5 - Let go of your past

You don't have to let go of everything, but if something happened that is keeping you stuck, I want to remind you that your past has zero bearing on your future. Holding on to what no longer serves you keeps you from creating a better future.

6 - Change how you think about yourself

Stop questioning your worth. You are worthy simply because you exist. If you find yourself thinking you're not good enough, recognize it and redirect your thoughts to your innate worth. Unleash this new perspective, and you'll open up a path to freedom you've never felt before.

7 - Never give up

When you have a dream or desire in your heart, you'll often have to endure discomfort. What I know now to be true is that withstanding this discomfort and showing up to do the hard things, even when you don't feel like it, is the path to your dreams. It's worth it.

8 - Rethink Time

Time is our most precious commodity. Instead of thinking you don't have time, pick up the habit of thinking you always have enough time. We each get to look at and decide how to think about time in any way that works for us. You have enough; however, you choose to spend it.

9 - Drop the manuals

We each have a manual for how we think people should behave, but it's exhausting to run someone else's life - not to mention impossible. Instead, bring the focus back to you. You get to be responsible for how you show up. Putting down these manuals lightens the burden.

10 - Get in the habit of thinking positively

Sometimes, we don't want to see things in a positive light, and that's okay, but I want you to know that it's available to you. There is such power in training your mind to look for the positive and be optimistic about the world.

These ten must-do habits will change your life for the better. You'll feel happier, lighter, and more at peace.

The Truth About Happiness

Happiness is something that everyone strives for. In fact, one of the biggest misunderstandings is the belief that life's goal is to always be happy. Yet, ironically, it's actually this thought that keeps us from being happy.

We must realize that happiness is a feeling and that our thoughts create our feelings - not any possession, person, activity, or amount of money.

It is so freeing and empowering to know it's always in your control. You don't have to wait for happiness. You just get to decide what makes you happy, and then you get to think about that.

But, to live your best human life, you don't want to be always happy. We are meant to have a plethora of feelings and experiences.

I like to picture a big serving platter, and being presented on this platter is a whole array of feelings and emotions. Yes, it would be easy only to select the "positive" emotions, but to have a balanced plate, you will want to include these other feelings and experiences in your life.

When you can feel any feeling and still understand that you are the creator of it all, then you're on the right track to living your highest, best life.

9

Overcoming Overwhelm

We often label our feelings as good or bad, positive or negative. But, what if instead, you think about all feelings being useful in how they will serve you to take action?

However, there are a few emotions that are actually not useful. These are often called "indulgent emotions" because they serve no purpose. They don't help you or increase your well-being in any way.

Overwhelm is one of these emotions.

When you're indulging in overwhelm, you don't have any traction for growth or movement. It can feel like it is necessary or important, but often, we don't do anything when we are feeling it. We use it as an excuse not to show up in our lives.

So, now that we know overwhelm doesn't serve us, here are some steps you can take to overcome it and make progress on the things that matter most to us.

1 - Stop and ask yourself, "Why am I feeling overwhelmed?"

Once you ask yourself this question, you can have your brain go to work for you instead of indulging in the emotion of overwhelm and staying there.

A great way to do this is to do a thought download. Write down all the thoughts you are having that are making you overwhelmed. There's so much swirling around in our heads; when you see those

DANIELLE THIENEL

thoughts on paper, you get to take the list out of your head! Then you can move on to the next step.

2 - Evaluate your list

Now that you have a complete picture of all the thoughts that are creating overwhelm for you, you get to evaluate them and see which ones are most pressing.

Take a moment and prioritize them, put them in order, and then see if there are some things you don't have to or don't want to do. Take those off your list and put the rest on your calendar. Then you don't have to think about that task until you get your reminder that it's time to do that.

3 - Take control over what you actually have control over

Once you've seen everything on your list, decide how you want to feel. If you no longer want to feel overwhelmed, you must think about things differently.

Whatever situation you are in, whatever your life circumstances are, you overcome them by becoming aware of everything you're thinking and then deciding what else you could think that feels better.

Your feelings don't depend on anything outside of you. Take responsibility for what you're feeling, recognize that staying overwhelmed won't serve you, and then take the steps to move beyond it and into emotions that will help you reach your goals.

10

I used to be able to argue a very good case of why perfectionism wasn't a bad thing and how seeking perfection had brought me many of the accomplishments that I was very proud of.

However, experience has now shown me that the pursuit of perfection is what kept me from living the peaceful life I desired for so long.

So, I want to ask you now, do you want to be perfect, or do you want to be peaceful?

If you said peaceful, here are three tools to help you get there:

1 - Learn to be satisfied with B- work.

If you consider the grading scale we grew up with in school, where an A equals excellence and an F equals failure, then learn to be okay with handing in work that would get you a B- grade.

Did you feed and bathe the kids but didn't have time to read every book they asked for? B- work.

Did you hope to make a homemade, nutritious sit-down meal for your family and managed a frozen pizza and a side salad instead of a baked-from-scratch lasagna? B- work

Is your house not spotless but clean enough? B- work.

You get the point. Aim high, but not so high it stops you from doing work that is good enough or from doing anything at all!

2 - Calendar your time and honor it

As a perfectionist, you likely have too many things on your to-do list that aren't getting done because they aren't good enough yet. The best thing you can do in this situation is to learn to complete your work in the allotted time – and then walk away when time is up. (Yes, even if it's not perfect yet!)

Choose an amount of time you think is reasonable for a task to take, and then show up and do whatever you said you would do. No matter what.

Here's the key: You MUST stick to the allotted time you assigned and then move on! Walk away when the time is up, even if the task isn't 100% finished. You'll learn to be okay with spelling mistakes and imperfections, knowing you can always come back to it another time.

3 - Understand your lovability

Perfectionists often fear being judged, disliked or seen as inadequate. Because of this, it's not uncommon for them to play small and stay stuck instead of pursuing their dreams.

What I have come to know and what serves me well on the path of perfectionism recovery is this: I am 100% worthy of love no matter what I do or do not do.

My lovability is infinite, and I am as loveable now as ever. It is not based on someone else loving me or how perfectly I perform.

No matter how "perfect" you are or how hard you try, you will inevitably miss the mark somehow. Instead of giving up or criticizing yourself, this is the time to choose self-compassion.

I used to think racking up a list of things I'd done perfectly would give me the peace I sought. But the arrival never comes. It's simply impossible to be perfect, so the perfect choice is to choose peace instead.

11

How To Stop Fighting With Your True Self

1 - Create the feeling of courage

Courage, like all feelings, is created by your thoughts. It will take courage to step out from the facade of your false self and live the life you were truly meant to. Not everyone will be supportive. It won't always be easy. But with courage, you can continue taking the next step toward your true self.

2 - Release old patterns and beliefs that no longer serve you

Uncovering these old patterns is a must because you can't change what you don't know. Not all old patterns or beliefs are bad or need to be changed, but some may be holding you back from living your true purpose. Some patterns used to serve you but no longer do. I benefited from hiring a coach to help me release these old patterns and beliefs.

3 - Tell the truth and align your decisions with your own personal truth

Sometimes, this is as simple as answering a question like, "If I wasn't going to be judged or disappoint someone else, what would I choose to do?" You are giving away your power when you do things to please others. When you say yes to them, you often say no to you and what you truly want. It's a lie! Begin instead to align your decisions with your truth.

4 - Develop yourself

Make it your life mission to learn something from everything you experience in life. Developing yourself allows you to tune into your inner wisdom more clearly and create a life that comes from your heart, a life that feels good on the inside and doesn't just look good on the outside.

5 - Go to your faith

Include God's presence in your plans. Ask for his help to stop saying yes when you mean no and for added courage to fight the false self. Ask Him to help you live out your authentic, true self.

Stop fighting with your true self and allow her to be set free.

12

Three Secrets About Emotional Wellness

1 - The goal of life is not to be happy all the time.

The truth is that to lead a full, robust life and have a complete earthly experience; you want to feel all kinds of emotions. When life presents a sad or difficult situation, we get to take charge of our emotional wellness by choosing how we want to feel.

There will be times when you want to feel sad, disappointed, hurt, or nervous. The key is recognizing that you are creating those feelings and knowing that you can choose to change your thoughts and get to the other side.

2 - Prioritizing yourself is not selfish.

To access that deep belief that you are a great mom, a good person, and a worthy child of God, you must take care of yourself.

When you are emotionally drained, you won't be able to feel and give love to the people in your life and enjoy all that you are creating. You won't be able to show up as the person you want to be. Allowing yourself time to fill back up your emotional reserves is one of the least selfish things you can do!

3 - You are responsible for all of your emotions.

If you feel anxious, overwhelmed, guilty, or hurt, blaming it on things outside of you won't be beneficial. You are the only one responsible for how you feel because you are choosing what you think.

But here's the good news, the joy, and peace you feel are also not caused by any outside circumstances. Instead, you feel joy and peace because of your thoughts.

So really, your emotional wellness is entirely in your hands. You get to create the level of wellness you desire at any time.

It's all up to you. Apply your personal power to love your life and live it in a way that serves you and the whole world.

13

The Powerful Habit of Peace

Like all feelings, peace isn't created when all our outside circumstances are lined up perfectly. Instead, peace is an internal job. It comes from the thoughts you choose to think about your life, creating feelings in your heart.

Circumstances will come and go in our lives - sometimes, they will be challenging, and sometimes they will be joyful. When we embrace the notion that troubles will come and go, we can gather our God-given power to create peace and remain peaceful despite the circumstances of our lives.

Cultivating the habit of peace is much like creating any practice. In the book Atomic Habits by James Clear, he outlines a simple process for creating a habit.

Step one is to decide what habit you want to create. In this case, you'd decide you will be a peaceful person. Step two is to prove it to yourself with small wins.

To start, bringing awareness to yourself and your current habits is essential. For example, would you consider yourself a peaceful person? If you reflect on the week, what percentage of the time would you say you felt peaceful?

Now that you know where you are starting, decide you want to be a peaceful person. This may not come naturally to you, but you can wake up each day and recommit to that decision to be peaceful.

Step two is to start taking small steps to reinforce this new, desired identity. Again, staying observant and directing your mind to the tiny wins is essential. Recognize all the little moments when you feel peace, and perhaps more importantly, acknowledge the moments where you wouldn't have felt peace in the past and now have been able to capture that peaceful feeling at the moment.

You can choose to start today having a peaceful mind and show up peacefully. Let it be a habit you focus on every day by deciding to step into this new identity and make small changes every day to reinforce this new peaceful way of life.

14

Whenever I feel stressed, out of sorts, confused, or worried, I return to some basic concepts. I call them the ABCs of Interior Peace.

A: Acceptance

Too often, we say things like, "I wish this wasn't happening" or "I wish this person didn't have this problem." Instead, we need to become aware of our current life and not argue with what is happening. Whatever your circumstances are, moving to a place of acceptance is the first step toward interior peace.

B: Boundaries

A boundary is something you create for yourself, not a way to control other people. It's a way of drawing a circle around our behavior and ourselves. This means you'll have to clearly communicate to others what you will and won't do. Are you setting healthy boundaries to maintain your interior peace? If not, look where you can and choose to follow through with them.

C: Courage

Courage has proved to be very important to my success in life and contributes to my internal peace. When your peace becomes an absolute priority and focus, you must be brave, step up, and take courageous action to make the necessary changes in your life. Your actions, coming from courage, will be profound.

D: Decision-Making

You'll have more peace when you focus on becoming a skillful decision-maker. When we don't make fast, strong decisions, we stay in confusion which is the opposite of peace. Look around your life, see where you feel confused, and begin making solid decisions today.

E: Embrace the Present Moment

When you aren't present, what's happening is that you are spending your mental energy in the past thinking about things that are over and done with or in the future thinking about things that could happen from a place of worry. Embracing the present moment is made possible when you redirect yourself to the now. Notice where your thoughts are and bring them back to the present moment for more peace.

F: Forgiveness

Forgiving ourselves and others are vital for internal peace. If you are reliving something and not letting go, it's affecting your present. Notice how your peace is disrupted by the mental anguish you're creating for yourself. It's time to let go and forgive.

G: Grace

This is a step that you can't do on your own. However, grace is essential and is something given to us from above. As humans, we don't get it right all the time. We're navigating, growing, and figuring out life without an instruction book. Know that you can call upon the grace of God to help you each day. Believe you will receive the peace you are looking for when you ask.

15

Blame and shame are some really sticky emotions. It's easy to get caught up in them. But, when we stop blaming our outside circumstances, we're no longer the victim of them.

Here are three tools I use when I find myself in blaming mode for taking back my power.

1 - Tell the whole truth

Ask yourself, "What is really the truth here?" Don't focus on what's happening with the other person, but ask yourself your role in the situation. What were you thinking and feeling that may have caused your present circumstances?

2 - Focus on what you have control over

Sometimes we find ourselves in a situation where we have to hold another person accountable for their actions. But the fuel we use to do this is so important. We give our power away when we hold people responsible from a place of blame. When we take our power back, we can make a positive difference. Instead of trying to control people, we can hold them accountable from a place of love and commitment.

3 - Drop the tug-of-war rope

When you are in a tug-of-war battle over who is right or wrong, I invite you to drop the rope. When you hold on, desperate for them

     DANIELLE THIENEL

to see it your way or to apologize, you are letting something that may never come control you. You deserve to have your peace and your power back. You don't have to agree with the other person to drop the rope, but choose to think thoughts that bring you more acceptance and peace.

16

Take a Break from Busy

Being busy is something we have made part of our identity as moms, but it doesn't have to be that way. "I'm busy" is not a fact, and it's something you can stop believing about yourself and your life today.

Here are three tools to help you take a break from busy.

1 - Recognize when you are operating on autopilot

When we take action from old thought patterns, we are moving at the effect of our brains. We are letting it run us. This lower part of our brain wants to keep everything easy, efficient, and status quo.

However, to take a break from busy, we can tap into the higher place in our brain - the prefrontal cortex. As a result, you can plan ahead of time with intention and purpose. And when you do plan in advance this way, you will take deliberate action that feels amazing.

2 - Stop people pleasing

Tap into the positive results and different energy you create when you believe you want to be doing something instead of having to do something. For example, let's say you volunteer to help with your child's field trip. If you do it because you believe that a "good" mom helps at her child's school, you may resent the other things you had to put aside that day.

Instead, when you stop adding things to your schedule that don't truly align with your priorities, you're creating more busy for yourself. Stop saying yes when you really mean no.

3 - Practice self-care

When moms feel better, everyone benefits. I love to use the analogy of a bucket to represent you, mamas. It's a beautiful bucket, but most of us have several holes in ours. And when there is a hole in the bucket, important things keep leaking out, and there isn't enough to give to others.

Self-care plugs the holes in your bucket. As you live your life and continue to do everything you want for your family, career, home, and faith, your bucket stays filled and overflows to all those around you. If you're not taking time for self-care, you're not being as effective as you could be as a wife and mother.

Satan loves to keep us thinking we're too busy. Why? Because preoccupation with events, tasks, and problems is a surefire way to distract us from trusting God and feeling at peace. Using these three tools to take a break from busy will create room for you to live an intentional life of joy, peace, and balance.

17

How To Stop Feeling Inadequate

Feelings of inadequacy can come up at any moment, especially if you're pushing yourself to go after those big dreams.

So here are some tips to help you believe in yourself, no matter what.

Tip 1: Picture yourself succeeding

It can be something simple like a meal you want to make or a hobby you've begun. It may be a business you want to start. Whatever you want to do that you feel too inadequate to start, I want you to stamp indelibly on your mind a mental picture of yourself succeeding.

This picture is something that you can hold and redirect your mind back to; as you do, your mind will go out and seek to develop that picture. That's what the brain does. It scans the world, and what you're focusing on will be drawn to you.

Tip 2: Voice a positive thought

Whenever a negative thought concerning your ability comes to mind, I want you to voice, out loud, a positive thought to cancel it out.

When a negative thought comes to mind or out of my mouth, I say, "cancel that!"

Our thoughts are our creation power. Therefore, the more you can be aware of your thoughts and keep them positive, the more positive results you can expect.

Tip Three: Understand your brain

When doing this kind of imagination exercise, your brain will come in and offer you all the obstacles to reaching your goal.

Instead of believing your brain, try to minimize the obstacles it is offering you, question them, and explore some things you can do to deal with them.

Look at these obstacles as what they are – thoughts. You can figure out a way to go through the challenges or have them disintegrate before you even meet them.

Tip Four: Focus on being the best you

Nobody can be you and do you as well as you do. When you forget that and compare yourself to others, you can have thoughts that trigger feelings of inadequacy. That feels terrible.

I want you to remember that we don't want to be copies of other people. I want you to focus on the qualities that no one else has. All you need to focus on is being the best you.

A scripture I love, Romans 8:31, has become a beneficial mantra to me when I'm hit with feelings of inadequacy.

It reads, "If God is for me, who can be against me?" It is so comforting and empowering to direct my mind here whenever it wants to tell me that I'm not good enough.

God is always for what we want in our hearts. He wants us to succeed, try, and know he's there to pick us up in the hard times.

I encourage you to try these tips the next time inadequacy comes into your heart or thoughts and bring yourself back to the power inside you.

18

The 50/50 Principle

When I was introduced to the 50/50 concept, I wasn't too sure. The 50/50 rule says that if you're living life to the fullest, using all your gifts, realizing your capabilities, and achieving your dreams, you will have 50% positive and 50% negative feelings.

I didn't want to have 50% negative feelings. I thought that the 10% I believed I was experiencing was plenty. But now that I know more, I realize that I wasn't living my life to the fullest by staying in a place where my life was 90/10.

When I loosened up to the idea of 50/50, I found myself stepping forward, putting myself in places where I could expand, grow, and go after things I never thought possible.

I often find that my clients have the misconception that we should always be happy and that if we aren't, something has gone wrong.

If you are always happy, that can tell you that perhaps you haven't tapped into your fullest potential and capability. You might be living a smaller life than God intended you to live.

But what if there is something else, something more you are made for?

We are on Earth to be challenged, grow, and become more like Christ. And to accomplish this, we must live a life as He had - with challenges, sorrow, and difficulty. He carried out his full mission before He ascended to heaven, and so should we.

Because this is an imperfect world, there will be difficult circumstances you'll have to face. That's okay! Step into those negative feelings and know they will bring you to a greater version of yourself.

Instead of avoiding feeling bad, we want to learn how to get good at feeling bad because it's just a feeling. Then, we can move through it to make ourselves better. View those hard things as an indicator that you're still on this side of heaven, and that's how it's meant to be.

19

Exquisite Self-Care

What would life look like if you gave yourself exquisite self-care? The definition of exquisite self-care is to take care of yourself in an extremely beautiful and delicate manner.

So, ask yourself, what would that look like for you? Would it look like weekly massages or getting your nails done? Does it have consistent time to curl up with a good book with no interruptions?

Is it spending focused time with your kids or going on a date with your husband? Is it going to bed half an hour earlier or waking up before your kids to exercise?

As moms, we deserve to take our self-care up a notch. And you must find a way because as you take care of yourself in this exquisite way, can you imagine how you will show up in your life and for your family?

What this exquisite self-care will look like will be different for each of us. It will depend on what stage of motherhood you are in and what your focus is on. But it's so important not to put off taking care of yourself until you hit rock bottom.

And, if you think that you don't know what to do, don't have the time, or can't find the money, raise your thoughts toward heaven and ask God, "How can I exquisitely start taking care of myself? Can you open a way? Can you give me ideas?"

As you take the time to take care of yourself, you'll find that you have more room to take care of others around you just as exquisitely as you care for yourself.

　　　　　　　　　　　　　　　DANIELLE THIENEL

20

Pivot to Peace

When confronted with a situation that leaves us feeling emotions other than peace, we can still choose to pivot to peace.

The first step is recognizing the situation for what it is - a neutral fact. Our circumstances don't hold any power over us. Our thoughts about these circumstances leave us with emotions like disappointment, fear, and anger or more positive emotions like acceptance, peace, and joy.

Sometimes in life, we will experience emotions that don't feel good. For example, you probably won't feel happy right away when a trip you were looking forward to is suddenly canceled. Instead, allow yourself to feel any emotion that circumstance brings up for you. You can feel an emotion and not react to it. As you sit with and process through that feeling, you'll find that it passes, and you'll be able to move into a new, more helpful emotion.

When you see what is in your control and what isn't, you can pivot to peace and access the power to make new decisions that allow you to enjoy life.

Just a slight pivot and adjustment can lead you to amazing results in your life.

21

The Need for Rest

We get so used to the conveyor belt of life, and we sometimes forget that we're not machines. Rest is necessary, and learning to unwind is a skill.

Directing your mind to a place of rest whenever possible is a crucial habit necessary to have the vitality and focus required to create the life we want. Rest is a basic need. We all know how important sleep is, but we also need to prioritize rest during our waking hours.

How much time and energy are wasted if we choose to always be on the go rather than taking the time to evaluate what matters in our lives and prioritize it accordingly? Sometimes, we aren't at rest, even when sitting on the couch, taking a walk, or driving in the car.

If you have spinning, swirling, constantly moving thoughts going in your mind, then you will never feel rested. However, when you learn to calm and quiet your mind, there can be rest inside you, even if chaos and turmoil are going on outside you.

Make time for rest. Make time for peace. Refuel yourself with downtime and moments to recharge purposely. Maybe that looks like focusing on scripture. It could be taking a walk and leaving your phone at home.

This intentional rest will recharge you and help you be a more effective mom, wife, and woman.

22

Five Secrets of Happy, Balanced Moms

As a mom, we want to be happy, we want to be joyful, and we also want to grow in our spiritual life.

These five secrets will help you navigate this life and deal with your problems while finding joy and abundant life.

Secret #1: Happy, balanced moms prioritize themselves.

When you put yourself first and prioritize yourself, that good can't help but spill over to all the others you come in contact with - your spouse, children, family, friends, and co-workers.

I know you want to take good care of your family, but you will only be the most effective mother, daughter, sister, friend, and faith-filled woman when you have prioritized yourself.

Let's stop making prioritizing ourselves a selfish thing. Instead, see it for what it truly is - when you're energized and fulfilled and have given yourself care and love, you will have much more to give to others.

Secret #2: Happy, balanced moms say no

We often worry about saying no because we think it's rude. But saying no is a beautiful thing. When you genuinely say no to something but don't, you are ultimately not being kind to yourself or the person you're saying yes to.

By saying no, you are setting an example of what it is to live out your truth. More often than not, a lot is being asked of you. You naturally want to be helpful, but what results is a negative outcome for you.

Happy, balanced moms know that saying no when you mean it leads to a more authentic and successful life.

Secret #3: Happy, balanced moms know that done is better than perfect

You shouldn't aim for A+ work in every area of your life. In fact, many times, B- work will be more than sufficient.

You want to aim high in life but not so high that it stops you from doing good enough work or anything.

Before you know it, you'll have accomplished far more than if you were still trying to make it perfect at the beginning. Remember, done is better than perfect.

Secret #4: Happy, balanced moms make time for what matters

Many things feel essential to do and take care of. However, there are only a few things that truly matter.

Time is just a mental construct that we put on ourselves. The thoughts in our minds convince us that we don't have enough time. It's not a fact or reality. What's so important is how we manage our minds around the construct of time.

You get to choose, direct, guide and assign meaning to your thoughts about your time, schedule, and how you feel about the things you're doing.

Satan loves to keep us thinking we're "too busy." Why? Because preoccupation with events, tasks, solving problems, and getting it all done is a surefire way to distract us from trusting God.

                                    DANIELLE THIENEL

But there is power within you to manage your time instead of time managing yourself.

Happy, balanced moms know there is an alternative to believing everything is essential. They learn to focus most of their time on just a few matters.

Secret #5: Happy, balanced moms talk to themselves as God would

You are a child of God and precious in his sight. Yet, we constantly talk to ourselves in a way opposite to what the Lord would say to us.

We are full of judgment and self-criticism and very good at piling lots of "should" onto ourselves. It can be equated to an internal radio dial that is always tuned to the station of negativity and criticism.

We often say things we would never say to a best friend or a loved one. So why do we think it's okay to say it to ourselves?

God sees you in your magnificence, with eyes of mercy, as his precious child, perfectly created in His image. He knows your humanness and loves you beyond understanding.

Happy, balanced moms remember this and speak to themselves as God would

23

Silently Suffering

When I work with the moms I coach, I'm no longer surprised when they tell me they have been silently struggling with a particular issue for years. They have some pain, struggle or challenge that they think negatively about. They have these thoughts repeatedly, and they begin to feel very true.

Is there something going on in your life that you believe you're the only one who has gone through it and that no one else would understand? Just stop and think how many billions of people are on the earth right now and how many have lived before us. Do you really believe there isn't anyone who hasn't gone through what you are?

And, even if, for some reason, you were the only person who had gone through this circumstance, God is always with you and knows everything about you. You can always talk to Him. There is no reason to suffer in silence.

When we have persistent thoughts and resist them, they persist. Being with the negative feelings, you're experiencing and allowing them, feeling them, lets them pass. When you allow your feelings, you open up, step into what's happening, and then examine what you have control over.

And, if your circumstances have you feeling isolated, can you choose to take some steps forward to get back into community? It could be chatting with someone at the grocery store or finding a group of people who can support you with the situation you're dealing with.

    DANIELLE THIENEL

When we take little steps, when we step our pain out loud, when we take small actions to find a community, we get out of the negative thought patterns we've been stuck in for so long.

It's okay to be scared, but let fear be in the passenger seat. Instead, put courage in the driver's seat and drive forward with courage. It takes courage to ask for help and reach out, but it is one of those magnificent risks we must take to change our lives.

24

Making Peace With Your Past

How do you use your past? Do you use it to move you forward, or does it keep you stuck and hold you back?

The truth is, your past no longer exists. It's over, and you can't change it. The past can't cause you suffering. It only affects you when you start thinking about it.

When you start thinking about the parts of your past you don't like, and it brings up negative feelings, know that it already happened and no longer exists. You have the choice to not think about it and have it affect your present moment.

Some people come to me really attached to their painful stories about their past. They talk about what should have been different, what wasn't fair, and what other people did in the past that caused hurt. Some circumstances are absolutely true that took place. We're not arguing with them. But the way you tell yourself the story matters.

You decide whether you are the hero of the story or the victim. You could believe that your past made you strong and capable and positively affected your life.

You can find a way to retell your story, and you don't have to take any of the parts you don't like with you. You can't change your past but can change what it means to you.

Your past successes and failures don't predict your future success or failures unless you believe they do. So I invite you to stop believing that the past has any bearing on your future. Instead, bring yourself back to all that matters - what you choose to think right now.

25

The Greatest of These is Love

What does it mean to love unconditionally? Love is an emotion you choose for yourself - regardless of how the other person behaves or what they choose.

You can choose to feel love for someone instead of anger or disappointment. Love isn't dependent on it being returned or even received by anyone.

Love feels good. It's an emotion that motivates positive and compassionate action. And when you are full of love for yourself, it's easier to give that love to others.

Whenever possible, choose love, and you'll find more peace.

26

Peace Restoring Tips

1 - Pray every day

Your prayer doesn't have to be long. It doesn't have to be structured. It just needs to be every day.

2 - Drop perfectionism

Make it your mission to recognize when you feel as if you have to be perfect. Then, instead of staying stuck there, move forward - even if it's not perfect, even if it's messy, even if it's wrong, even if it's embarrassing, even if you're judged for it - because that's how you make progress.

3 - Forgive yourself

It's constant work to get to the place in our life where we want to be. So instead of spending time beating yourself up about your mistake, use that energy to practice forgiving yourself.

4 - Love where you are

Bring awareness and gratitude to what's going on in your life, even if you wish it weren't. You can love the present. Look for what's good in what's happening. That is where your power lies.

5 - Let go of your past

Your past has zero bearing on your future. It's done and over, so holding on to the parts of your past that aren't serving you is holding you back from creating a better future.

6 - Change how you think about yourself

I never want you to question your worth again. You are worthy simply because you exist. You are worthy of it all. You are here to enjoy and have an abundant life.

7 - Never give up

Know that withstanding discomfort and showing up to do the hard things, even when you don't feel like it is the path to your dreams. It's worth it.

8 - Rethink Time

Instead of thinking that you don't have enough time or have too much to do, pick up the habit of thinking you always have enough time. We each get to look at and decide to think about time in any way that works for us. You have enough; however, you choose to spend it.

9 - Drop the manuals

We each have a manual for how we think other people should behave, but it's exhausting to run someone else's life. Not to mention impossible! Instead, bring the focus back to you and give others the freedom to show up how they choose to.

10 - Get in the habit of thinking positively

We can choose to enjoy this journey. You can choose thoughts that bring on positive feelings. It's just more fun, easier, and more light-hearted. There is such power in training your mind to look for the positive and be optimistic about the world.

27

Clean Parenting

Parenting is something I talk a lot about with my clients. And with good reason! It's one of the most important and long-lasting things we do in our lives.

Here are some actionable steps that you can use to become a more peaceful parent.

Peace With The Past

The first vital step in peaceful parenting is to go down memory lane and see how you are currently writing the story of your past. Next, you want to know if you are looking at your past parenting in the most favorable light you can muster.

What do you think about your parenting? How are you speaking about it? What are you telling yourself and others? Are those things being considered or talked about in a way that serves you and brings you peace now?

If not, I want you to consider letting go of what you didn't like about your past parenting. Forgive and forget the mistakes you think you made as a parent. Stop bringing yourself suffering over things that can't be changed. Those things were actually supposed to happen because they did happen.

Then, you get to work at rewriting and retelling yourself the story of your past parenting in a way that brings you feelings of peace instead of regret. The past can't be changed, and wanting things to be different only brings you pain now.

 DANIELLE THIENEL

Whatever we tell ourselves about how we acted up until now, the details about what took place in our past up until this point is on us. We make it mean something based on how we look at it and the story we tell ourselves.

Start telling yourself a different story about it all!

Keep all the good parts. Remember how you made every doctor's visit or wrote down all the milestones? Remember how you prayed over them when they were sleeping or drove them to thousands of athletic practices?

Look at each chapter of your story and remind yourself that you did the best you could with what you knew then. Your heart desires to be the best parent. However, you are human with frailties and misgivings too. Yet, you continued to learn and try again.

So, I ask you to release the things you have done in the past and rethink them in a new way. The new story is what matters now.

Peace In The Present

The second step is to choose peaceful thoughts about your parenting amid your current circumstance.

Whatever stage of parenting you are in right now, with whatever age children you have, and whatever your situation may be, how you think about it all right now will bring you peace.

How can you believe you are doing a great job as a parent? You simply ask your brain to look for evidence that you are a great parent. Try it!

The answer might be something like

- You fed your kids today.

- You gave them a hug and a kiss.

- You prayed for them this morning.

- You played a game with them.

- You didn't lose your temper when they didn't listen the first time.

- You care about their day and ask them about it.

- You give them a safe place to talk.

This list could go on and on.

Thinking this way will give you a feeling of peace about your parenting. Focusing on your mistakes doesn't bring you peace, and it doesn't motivate you to change. You get to choose where you focus.

Peace In The Future

The third vital step is to choose to think positively about the future.

Do you see a future you like? Do you believe your kids will turn out fine? Or do you think about the future and feel worried?

I want to invite you to choose to believe that all will be well. I encourage you to let your imagination work hard to create a picture that brings you peace. See your children thriving and being wonderful human beings in the world. Picture them married to great spouses. Picture those grandbabies and step into the parent you want to be in the future.

Instead of worrying about what might be, purposefully generate peace about the future. The challenges that the future may hold are meant to be felt and experienced later when they happen.

What you think now will ultimately create the results you get in the future.

If you believe things like, "I may ruin my kids," "I'm not setting a good enough example," or "They might get hurt or take the wrong path," it instills feelings of doubt, worry, and guilt.

From those negative feelings, you'll create a future full of results that loop around to bring you more worry, doubt, and guilt.

Instead, look at how you want to feel about your job as a parent, no matter what the future brings.

The future is yet to be written.

Believe that you'll raise amazingly successful kids. Believe you will give them all they need to be the wonder God created them to be.

Remember that your job is to do the best you can with the time you have with them. God is in control of the future. Trust that he will help you and help your children when the time comes.

The most wonderful part of all of this is the choice we have to feel at peace about our past, present, and future. You don't have to wait to feel peace. You can think peaceful thoughts about your past and future while being peaceful in the present.

28

Enjoy the Journey

When people come to me, they usually want help to achieve something. For example, they may want a stronger marriage, a better job, or to carve out time for more self-care.

There are so many things that we juggle. We have many wishes for our families and our own lives. And then we get overwhelmed and don't know where to start.

But there is one misconception that I want to address today - there is no need to delay enjoyment!

If we are constantly telling ourselves we have to wait to feel joy until we have accomplished something, it will be too late. We don't get the time back.

Once you achieve your goal, you may feel joy. But why would you want to put off feeling that joy until you reach a specific destination? What do you gain from your life if you hold off feeling joy and happiness?

Joy is all around us. We don't want to wait for something outside us to bring it to us. We can create that joy for ourselves when we direct our brain to think thoughts that make us happy and joyful.

We need to enjoy the journey. When you are not enjoying it, notice that and bring yourself back into your power. Start today enjoying your one and only life. Find something good every day as you travel to your goals.

Do not conform yourselves to this age
but be transformed by the renewal of your
mind, that you may discern what is the
will of God, what is good and
pleasing and perfect.
-Romans 12:2

29

The Power Of Questions

We ask ourselves questions all day long. What am I going to wear today? When will I stop feeling so exhausted? Why is life so hard right now?

In coaching, however, questions are the tools we use to change lives for the better. We use them to help you become aware of your thoughts, which is everything!

The thoughts in your mind create your life. Asking yourself high-quality, empowering questions opens you to creativity and inspiration to create the awesome life God wants you to live.

Ask yourself, "What do I really want?" and the brain will go looking. Ask yourself, "How can I be happier?" Your brain will come back with wonderful ideas. You'll find a source of wisdom within you that you might not have known existed.

When you call on the power of questions, you'll find the answers are all inside you.

30

You Are Not Your Thoughts

You are a complete, whole, worthy, perfectly created human being. You have a 100% loveable and perfect soul in The Creator's eyes. That soul is separate from your mind, with ideas, notions, sentences, and phrases coming and going.

Experts say we have between 6 to 8 thousand thoughts each day. Sometimes they are lightning fast, and we never realize they passed through our mind, and other times we think a thought so often it becomes part of our belief system.

Pausing to notice and zoom out will help you distinguish that you are not your thoughts - you are the watcher of your thoughts.

This distinction is so important because this means you have the power to change how you feel just by noticing what you're thinking.

Knowing that you are not your thoughts is a huge step toward having a peaceful mind and creating all the great things you want for your life.

31

The Best News Ever

Are you ready for the best news ever?

You get to choose what you think - every moment, every day. There is never a moment when the choice isn't yours.

You are in control of assigning meaning to everything - how you mother, what has happened in the past, what you think about your kids, your friends, your job, and your faith. You choose what to think about all of it!

What do you want to think about how much time you have? What do you want to think about your parenting? What do you want to think about your relationship with Christ?

Your mind is full of thoughts, some of them negative, some positive, and some just indulgent and not useful. You can create an amazing life by choosing thoughts that serve you on purpose so often that they become true beliefs to you.

You get to write your own story and choose what you want to think about everything. This is the work, my friends. The work that leads you closer to a peaceful mind.

32

Thoughts To Think On Purpose For
A More Peaceful Mind

- I am guided.
- Everything is as it should be.
- Everything happens for me.
- It was meant to happen the way that it did.
- I am exactly as I should be.
- Everything happens right on time.
- God doesn't make mistakes.
- I am not my mind. I am the watcher of my mind.
- Love is always an option.
- Unconditional love is something I do for myself.
- I'm responsible for everything I think and feel.
- No one can cause an emotion inside of me.
- People are allowed to behave the way they want. I am allowed to react the way I want.
- It's not what I do; it's who I am.
- There's nothing I can do that wouldn't be worthy of forgiveness.
- There's nothing wrong with me.
- I am enough.
- Nothing has gone wrong here.

- I am simply worthy because I exist.
- My purpose is the life I am living right now.
- I am deeply loved.
- The world longs for what I have to offer.
- There's nothing that you truly want that you cannot have.
- Hard work feels amazing.
- I can do hard things through Christ who strengthens me.
- Suffering is sometimes familiar, but it's not necessary.
- Worry serves no purpose.
- Money is easy.
- I am meant for abundance.
- There is plenty of time.
- God is for me, so there's nothing against me.
- Everything I do is a choice.
- My past is perfect.
- There's nothing they can do to make me happy. That's my job.
- What I do doesn't make me happy. What I think does.
- I am fun.
- What I look for, I will find.
- What others think of me is about them, not me.

33

What Are Circumstances?

Circumstances are things outside of our control. For example, this includes other people, our past, and the weather.

Sometimes we forget that we can't control these things. So we expend all our energy trying to control other people or change our past. But it never works.

Circumstances are also facts. They could be proven in a court of law. Everyone would agree that they are true.

So your child misbehaving isn't a circumstance. Not everyone would agree that your child's behavior is unacceptable. So it's not a fact.

Often we think we are relaying facts, but they are, in fact, the thoughts in our minds instead.

The most important thing to remember about circumstances is that they are neutral. They can't cause you any harm until your mind enters the chat. That is where you attach meaning to your circumstances.

This matters because when you realize your mind causes your feelings, you can be much more in control of your emotional life. Of course, it doesn't mean you don't choose to be sad or mad, but you will be aware that you are the creator of it, not your circumstances.

For too many of us, our own stories are painful and even debilitating, keeping us stuck and spinning in doubt. This is where we want to separate the circumstances from the thoughts and stories we've been telling ourselves.

When we realize something is a circumstance, it becomes a data point. It is just a fact in the world, and now you can choose what you think about it and what you make it mean.

And that is where all the power lies.

34

The Power of Thoughts

Thoughts are the main tool I use to help moms find more peace and balance. Thoughts are my favorite!

Because the thoughts you think are the cause of everything you create in your life!

When someone presents a challenge or struggle to me, I know it will ultimately come down to a thought that they are thinking that is creating that challenge or struggle for them.

We think a lot of thoughts in a day. I've seen estimates anywhere between 6,000 to 10,000 a day. And out of those thousands of thoughts, 95% of them are unconscious.

Whenever you think of something new, it creates a weak neural pathway in your brain. And, if you keep repeating that thought over and over, and add emotion to it, then it becomes more and more unconscious and effortless.

So the first thing to do is to become aware of what you are thinking. Take pen to paper and preface it with the question, "What am I thinking right now?" It's very powerful to turn the intangible object of a thought into something you can actually see.

Then, you can look at each thought individually and ask questions like

- Do I like that thought?

- Do I want to keep thinking it?

- Do I want this thought to become a strong belief?

- Does it serve me well?

If the answer is yes, great! But, we want to become conscious of the thoughts that we recognize as self-critical or negative. And there's nothing wrong with having those either, but we want to be sure we are choosing them on purpose.

As humans, we give meaning to our circumstances through our thoughts. We can't always change our circumstances, but we can change our thoughts about them.

Our thoughts influence our behavior and directly affect the experience we are having. So, what you are currently thinking about is creating your life.

Your thoughts matter. Your mindset, what your brain is choosing to think again and again about the world, your life, yourself, your motherhood, everything, is all of supreme importance.

God gave us this tool of thoughts to co-create our lives with Him. Harness the power of your thoughts and take control of your creation power.

35

Where Do Feelings REALLY Come From?

Feelings are important because they are behind everything we do or don't do.

However, a feeling is simply an emotion or vibration we experience in our bodies. It's important to understand the difference between a feeling and a sensation. Sensations are involuntary, and they start in the body. Feelings or emotions start in the brain, and they are a vibration we experience in the body and are caused by what we think.

We often think feelings come from our circumstances. We say things like, "My husband doesn't take out the trash, so I feel angry." Or we say, "My best friend is in town, so I'm very excited!"

But feelings actually come from our thoughts about our circumstances.

We all have hopes and desires for ourselves and the people around us. We love our families, and we want so much for them. We dream of how our lives and their lives can be. But the truth is, we really want the feelings we believe we will have once we get everything we're thinking or dreaming about.

So take a moment and think about what you want. Then ask yourself how you believe you'll feel when you get what you want.

The great news is that we get to choose our thoughts, and we can choose a thought that brings on those feelings. You are the only one who can choose what you think.

If you want to change your life, you must become aware of what you're feeling in the present moment. Can you name what you're feeling right now? Do you know where that feeling shows up in your body?

When you realize that the worst thing that can happen is you will feel an emotion, you begin to understand that you don't need to resist things anymore. You might feel embarrassment, fear, or vulnerability, but it's just a feeling!

It might be uncomfortable, but knowing you can handle any feeling and change that feeling by thinking differently gives you so much power! Sometimes stepping into those negative feelings is the path to creating your dreams.

Understanding how your feelings are created will help you drive the actions you want to make the life you want.

36

Healthy-Mindedness

Healthy-mindedness is one of the greatest blessings in the world, but it takes some work. However, that work is well worth it because every experience you've ever had, every emotion you've felt, every goal you've set and achieved, and everything you've created for yourself comes from your mind.

When you have a healthy mind, you become a well-balanced, integrated, and well-organized human. You're devoid of inner conflict and obsessive reactions. The emotional aspect of your nature is under control. You are free from fear and hate. You're not motivated by resentment.

You will still have necessary human experiences in this life, like feeling disappointed, sad, or frustrated. But when you have these emotions, you will know they aren't a problem - they are just part of the human experience. Life is supposed to be challenging in ways that allow us to grow and make us better.

We often focus on ensuring our bodies are physically healthy. We spend time and energy preparing healthy meals. We spend money on fitness programs or gym passes to increase our endurance and strength. But are you spending the same effort, time, and money on improving your mental and emotional health?

A healthy body is a wonderful and crucial thing, but a healthy mind is equally (if not more) critical. Our brain is the greatest creation tool we've been given!

The most significant work I have done on my brain started with an awareness of where and how I was spending my mental energy. And once I realized I was the creator of my experience by what I chose to believe, I saw what was possible for me, and I began investing time, energy, and money in my mind.

Learning how to have a healthy mental life is crucial for seeing the good and seeking good outcomes, even when it doesn't seem like anything is going right.

This is exercising our faith muscles. Choosing to do the curious and fun work of learning to handle any circumstance that comes our way and feel what you want to feel, no matter what life throws at you, takes healthy-mindedness.

37

When To Talk More Than You Listen

We've been taught the importance of listening our whole lives, but there is a time when it's more important to talk more than you listen: when you're talking to yourself!

We have constant chatter going on in our minds. We think thousands and thousands of thoughts a day. We have sentences and phrases that come in and come out. Some of them stick and stay there for a while.

Our brain is a fantastic thing, but if we don't step in to intentionally direct it, we won't be able to live up to our highest potential.

When we start tapping into our higher brain and talking to ourselves deliberately, saying things like

- I'm an amazing mom.
- I can do hard things.
- I've got this!
- What do I need today?
- What can I do today to serve my family?
- I am amazing!
- There is no one else like me!
- I am meant to be my kids' mom.

When it comes to negative self-criticism, we must stop listening and start talking back. Our brains can't talk and listen simultaneously, so start talking!

Talk to yourself as God would. He would be your biggest cheerleader. You've got this!

38

When you see someone who has something you want to achieve, instead of feeling discouraged or that you are less than them, you can investigate what they might have been thinking that allowed them to reach their goal.

Sometimes you'll be in a position where you can ask them what they thought while they were on their journey to their goals, and other times, you might have to take a guess.

Once you have an idea of the thoughts they used, you can choose to borrow them for your own life. This might feel uncomfortable to you at first. Learning to believe new thoughts will take focus, practice, and work to get there.

You achieve new results as you believe this new thought pattern and tell a new story of your life and what's possible. As you shift to and gain a different energy, vibration, and feeling that drives the actions that help you reach your goals.

39

Peace Around Money

What do you believe about money?

Do you think that it's abundant? Is it easy for you? Do you work hard for money? Do you believe you never have enough?

The way you think about money will determine how much you have.

The first step is separating the facts of your situation from your thoughts about them. The math of your money is the situation you're in. It's your circumstance. It is neutral.

Next, you must look to our past for times when money has worked out for us. Perhaps you're considering purchasing something and are hesitant or afraid because it feels too risky or expensive. Dive into the past and look for another time when you felt these feelings and everything worked out.

Sometimes God requires us to jump, and then the parachute of God providing opens. One example is when we sent our twin girls to a private school, and it felt costly. I didn't have peace around the cost of it, but I had a lot of peace about providing the experiences I wanted for my kids.

I went with faith and jumped off the cliff. I worried about how we would pay for it or what would happen if we had to take them out because we couldn't afford it, but God came through and provided for us then and every year after.

Maybe your experience was when you were in college, deciding to stay home with your kids or investing in a business. Where has it always worked out? Knowing that today is no different than back then will allow you more peace around money.

And last, when it comes to anything in life, what you focus on grows. So if you want to focus on having more money or feeling better about money, then where should you focus?

Are you asking your brain questions like, "How can I get more money?" or "How can I grow as a steward in the money I have?"

The analogy I like to use is to imagine a patch of grass that you're standing over with a hose. The hose is pouring out water, and because you are directing it on this patch of grass, it's growing lush and thick. But, on the other hand, the patch of water you aren't watering is sparse and brown.

Expanding our thoughts about money to those bringing peace will require focus and attention. Get clear on those thoughts and generate more good feelings about money, especially peace.

As you do this, you'll find less worry, doubt, lack, scarcity, and confusion. You'll feel more peace about money, and those good feelings will attract more things you want.

40

Believing New Things

Believing in new things is imperative to reach your goals and creating extraordinary results. So whether you're a mom struggling with managing your time, one that's about to get back into the workforce, one who is ready to start a side gig or struggling with your marriage, organizing your home, or building confidence, believing new thoughts is the first step.

So here is the process for believing a new thought:

1 - Understand that everything starts in your brain

Everything that has ever been created started in someone's brain first. It's time to stop being unconscious about what we think and being intentional. As the watcher of your thoughts, you can become aware of what you're creating with your thoughts.

A brain dump is a great first step. Once you get all your thoughts on paper, you can see the tangible thoughts you are thinking and how those thoughts create your actions and results.

2 - Accept that what you believe is based on your past.

Your brain is filled with sentences that were taught to you directly or indirectly throughout your life. Some of them are so ingrained that you don't notice them anymore. They feel as though they are the truth, but they really are just thoughts.

When we start to question them, there will be some that have served us. You feel good when you think of them and want to hold onto them. But there will be others that you want to leave behind. The key is to pay close attention to your thoughts. The reason you have them might feel justified, but some thoughts don't get you closer to where you want to be.

3 - Choose to believe a new thought

You have complete control over where your mind focuses. It will take intention and practice, but it's nothing you haven't done before. You've been practicing certain thoughts your whole life, some positive and some negative. So now, when trying to believe new thoughts, we have to do the same thing, but with thoughts, we choose on purpose.

Choose your new belief. There are no rules about what you can and can't believe. You don't need any outside approval. You can decide to believe that you're amazing, a great mom, beautiful, very organized, a great time manager, or that you've got it all under control. You can believe anything you want and then get to work proving this true to yourself.

4 - When your beliefs change, you create change

Our brain can't believe two opposing thoughts simultaneously, so you must choose what you want to think deliberately. I like to have my clients use their imagination to picture what it will look like when they are the person who has reached their goal. What does it look like? What are you doing? What are you thinking? How are you feeling? What does it look like when you get up in the morning or go to bed at night?

Tap into your imagination. Start to visualize what it will look like. When we hold onto that picture, our brain will go to work helping us make that vision a reality.

Keep following this process of choosing new thoughts as often as you can. Over time, it will become second nature, and you'll find yourself creating your desired results.

 DANIELLE THIENEL

41

Is the voice in your head your best friend or your worst bully? When you gain awareness of the thoughts constantly going on in your head, you may be surprised how often you talk to yourself with words you would never say to your best friend (or even your worst enemy).

Think of your best friend. Picture them and think of all the times you've spent together. Think of the times when things weren't so great in your life and how your friend showed up for you.

If you acted like your own best friend, what kind of things would you say to yourself? This is where we want to stay most of the time - supported, accountable, uplifted, inspired, and loved.

The opposite of this is our bully brain. Unfortunately, I know far too many mamas constantly living with a bully brain telling them they aren't good enough, that they'll never figure it out, or that they might as well stop trying.

But bullying ourselves is never the way to make a change. Just like you'd never tell your best friend they were a failure to motivate them to do something, you need to change how you think about yourself to bring out your best.

Bring awareness to the way you are talking to yourself. When you hear that bully brain start, talk back to it. Treat yourself with compassion and love, and I promise you'll start seeing more results in your life that you want and love.

42

Creating More Time

Time is our more valuable asset. But how our minds look at time often hinders us instead of helping us lead a life full of what matters most to each of us. We think there will never be enough time, we have so much to do, and we will never get it all done.

But is this really true?

Time doesn't change, but the way you think about it will change your experience of time.

Time is just a mental construct we humans have put upon ourselves. It's the thoughts in our minds that convince us we don't have enough time, not a fact of reality. How we manage ourselves and our minds within that earthly construct is important.

You get to choose, direct, guide, and assign meaning to all thoughts you think about your time, your schedule, what's happening in your day, whether it's enough or not enough, how you're spending each moment, and how you feel about each thing you're doing.

You have far more control over utilizing your time than you've ever let yourself believe.

To expand our time and stay in line with our values, we must frequently reevaluate how we spend our time.

When our schedules are full, it's easy to convince ourselves that every event on the calendar and every task on the list is vital. And if we believe that thought, we likely feel overwhelmed, tired, frustrated, and trapped. The alternative to that belief is that just a few things matter.

I recommend writing down everything you are currently doing to find what truly matters. Then make a list of the things that are important to you. Then it's time to evaluate if what you're currently doing matches up with your priorities. Are there any tasks, events, commitments, or responsibilities you can let go of that don't align with your priorities?

When you are only doing the things that really matter to you and that you are intentionally choosing to do, you'll begin to feel that you have an abundance of time.

Be on to yourself when you don't have enough time. Catch yourself feeling that way, and remember it's a choice.

Choose deliberately how you'll spend your time and then grow in your belief that what you're doing with your time aligns with your highest self, and you'll find yourself feeling more productive and at peace.

43

Thoughts to Overcome Perfectionism

No matter how "perfect" you are or how hard you try, you will inevitably miss the mark somehow.

Perfectionists often fear being judged, disliked, or seen as inadequate. Because of this, it's not uncommon for them to play small and stay stuck instead of pursuing their dreams.

What I have come to know and what serves me well on the path of perfectionism recovery is this: I am 100% worthy of love no matter what I do or do not do.

My lovability is infinite, and I am as lovable now as I ever will be.

It is not based on someone else loving me or how perfectly I perform.

This is one thought that has helped me in my journey to overcome my perfectionist tendencies. Here are more that might be useful for you:

- Almost perfect is perfect for me.
- This can be meaningful without being perfect.
- I'm figuring this out.
- Failure is the learning path to success.
- Done is better than perfect.
- I make more progress when it doesn't have to be perfect.

44

The Belief Scale

Whenever you want to check where you are in your mind management, you can ask yourself a simple question and rate your response on a scale of 1-10. It could go something like this, "On a scale of 1-10, how happy am I?

Pick a number, and then answer why you picked that number. The reason why you picked that number will tell you all the thoughts you are having that are creating that level of happiness. Then ask yourself the question, what would I need to think to be at a 10 out of 10? When you answer that, you'll get all the thoughts that will help you create moving toward that greater joy.

This tool is a brilliant way to discover where your mind and heart are. This moment matters because the present moment and what you choose to think about, how you are feeling, and what you are doing or not doing is creating everything in your future.

When you deliberately choose to think the thoughts that will help you move forward to create the ultimate goals you have for yourself, you'll get to where you want to be.

...but those who hope in the Lord will renew their strength. They will soar on wings like eagles; they will run and not grow weary, walk, and not be faint.

-Isaiah 40:31

45

Light in the Darkness

We will all experience dark places throughout our lives. Sometimes it will be a short spurt, and other times it will be for a longer period. But, we have the choice of what we choose to focus on.

If you focus on the darkness and imagine it growing, it will. Procrastination, self-destructive behaviors, and staying stuck in the past all contribute to the growing darkness.

But we can also choose to focus on the light and allow it to grow. Prayer, reflection, and drawing on memories that are good and positive can all help the light grow.

Even when the light is just a tiny sliver, you can focus on it and help it to grow.

This won't always be easy, especially if you've been in this negative pattern for a while. But just like going to the gym to get stronger, the more you practice redirecting your brain to the good, the easier it gets.

46

The Truth About Worry

Our society has led us to believe that worry is a badge of honor, but I want you to consider that worry is simply a mental habit you've adopted.

It seems important to worry. It may even feel justified. But really, worry is an indulgent emotion that keeps us from taking action. You find yourself at the mercy of your life's circumstances. You spend time being reactive or resisting what you can't control and avoid doing something that would enhance your life.

Worry never changes the future. It only changes your now.

So when you are in the midst of motherhood and worrying about a list of things, think about this: what is it costing you?

Worrying keeps you stuck from accessing your inner knowing. It keeps you from finding a solution and taking better actions.

Worrying turns you away from practicing the muscle of trusting God's plan. When your mind is full of God, there is no room for worry. And with God's help, you can change any habit, including a mindset of worry.

Worry is useless, but building your trust in God will always prove fruitful.

47

Transforming Trials Into Blessings

We all have trials in this human life. Things will happen that are out of our control and that we wish weren't happening. And sometimes, life will present us with a hardship that we want to be sad, angry, disappointed, or frustrated about. You don't have to be happy about everything that comes your way.

But what I want to offer you is that when you ask your brain a powerful, positive question, it looks for powerful, positive answers.

So, amid any trial, I invite you to ask, "How will this be perfect for my life?" This is a tool I use to help move me closer to accepting the circumstances I find myself in.

When we accept and know there will be hard times, having this question in your back pocket will provide you with a total mind shift and a laser-focused way of putting your mind to use for you.

There are always blessings to be found when we look for them, but we have to redirect our minds and transform any trial to fit our definition of a blessing.

I promise you that if you focus on blessings, look for blessings, expect blessings, and get curious about how something is a blessing; your brain will seek and find a blessing there.

  DANIELLE THIENEL

48

5 Questions to Prevent Burnout

1 - Do I really want to be doing this?

A lot of times, we're doing things because we think we're supposed to do them. Take time to evaluate the things you're doing and question them. This doesn't mean you don't do anything hard. Sometimes you'll choose to do those hard things because of what they give you. But, if you don't want to be doing something, either stop doing it entirely or find a way to hand it off to someone else.

2 - Does it really matter to me?

When we are energized by what we're doing, we don't get burned out. Evaluate the things you are doing in your life, try to do more things that matter to you, and reevaluate the importance of the things that leave you feeling drained.

3 - How could this be easy?

We all have goals and dreams, but when I reach for one, I love to think, "how could this be easy?" Is there a way to use your brain to figure out a different process for what you're doing? When we ask our brain a high-quality question, it looks for an answer, so don't be surprised when ideas come just by asking yourself this question.

4 - How can I make it more fun

Less fun = more burnout. It's essential to consciously and consistently make an effort to add more fun to your life. You need fun. You need laughter. You need rest. Sometimes we have to get to the work at hand, but we can move our brain to a different, more relaxed state when we focus on making tasks fun.

5 - Does it serve my family and me?

Sometimes as moms, we get bogged down in day-to-day tasks. But, when we believe what we are doing benefits our family, it fuels us up. Serving the people who matter to you feels good! Celebrate all the good you are doing. Recognize yourself for all the amazing things you do to make a great life for yourself and your family.

49

How Not To Worry (for very long)

Are you a mom who worries about everything? Are you constantly worrying about your life, kids, or decisions? Here are some steps you can take to slow down worrying and not make it such a big part of your life.

1 - Recognize that worry is a feeling.

Our thoughts cause all our feelings; in this case, our thoughts trigger the feeling of worry. When we understand this, we know that we have created this emotion for ourselves, not our outside circumstances. We can get traction over it and choose whether we want to stay in worry.

2 - Understand that worry isn't preventative

When we worry, our brain is convinced there is an emergency and that the only option is to worry. But worrying doesn't serve you in any way. It's not preventative. If anything, you are causing yourself to feel a negative emotion twice about something that may or may not happen in the future. So when you are consumed with worry, remember it doesn't prevent anything. In fact, it prevents you from accessing your inner wisdom and problem-solving skills

3 - Know that worry lives in the future.

When you are worried, it means you aren't in the present moment. Worry lives in the future, telling us of something that might happen. So when you find yourself worrying, remember that you are in the present moment, not the future. In the present moment is where all your power lies.

These three reminders can help you stop worrying (for very long) and allow you to live a calmer life. You'll find yourself taking better actions when you come from a place of peace rather than worry.

50

How To Stop Feeling Guilty

Guilt is a normal human emotion. Our lower brain will always try to talk us into feeling bad about ourselves. But while guilt may be normal, the number one thing I want you to know is that feeling guilty is not serving you in any way!

There is a false notion that guilt helps you do better. But here's the thing: guilt is an indulgent emotion that actually keeps you stuck.

So, how do we stop feeling guilty?

First, we need to recognize what is a circumstance and what is truly our thinking about that circumstance.

It is ALWAYS your thoughts that are causing the feelings of guilt.

So, if we want to stop feeling guilty, we have to realize the true cause of guilt is self-imposed.

Instead of staying in the guilt cycle, can we open ourselves up to see other things that are just as true?

Some examples of thoughts could be:

- There I go being human again.
- Moms get frustrated sometimes.
- I don't have to be perfect to be worthy.

There are other options that don't create guilt for you!

Remember, guilt always stops progression. It will always keep you stuck. It doesn't serve you, your family, or anyone you care about.

I would like to challenge you to make it your mission not to stay in guilt.

Find whatever it is you need to think about so that you can feel better and take action that gives you a result you want instead of one that keeps you stuck.

That is how we genuinely improve and show up better each day.

51

How To Stop Yelling

Often, we beat ourselves up as mothers because we never pictured ourselves raising our voices to our children, yet here we are. So, how do you stop yelling?

First, you have to realize you're not broken. We have this idea that the perfect mom never yells but ask yourself, is that true? Can you be an amazing mother and still yell sometimes?

I would like to offer that the answer to that is yes. It can be a fantastic gift to show our children that we are human and model the process of apologizing for them.

Next, we have to get curious about what triggers us. What would you list as the top five triggers that cause you to yell?

Then, we need to identify what we are thinking about those situations. It is important to get to the root of what you're feeling and the thoughts behind it.

For me, stress is one of the emotions that causes me to yell. It's not typically even about the kids. Maybe we're running late getting out the door. Perhaps I'm worried about something else on my plate and haven't been getting great sleep. Maybe the house is messy, and I'm thinking overwhelming thoughts about getting everything done.

Regardless, it's not about the circumstances, and it's always about our thoughts about the circumstances.

When you practice thoughts that lead you to feelings of calm, peace, or acceptance such as, "This is what children do," you can show up from a better place. Instead of defaulting to a reaction of yelling, you can respond intentionally.

Be patient with yourself as you break patterns you have created over time. It may not happen overnight. But asking yourself how you want to do things differently moving forward means it only matters what you are thinking and believing about yourself now and what actions those things will motivate you to take moving forward.

52

3 Motherhood Myths

1 - You need to be a better mom

It's a myth that you need to be any better than you are right now. We all have things that we want to change, but what if we spent at least equal time listing all the things that we are doing right? Send your mind to find all the things that you do that are great, that serve your family, and that make you a great mom.

Here's a little secret: you can just decide you are a great mom. You don't need anyone to tell you or to check certain things off a list to prove it. You can just decide you are a great mom and leave it at that.

2 - You should put your family first

We've been taught we should put our family first and ourselves lower on the list. But, when you think about how it works, this logic starts to appear a little faulty. If you put your family first all the time, what will you be thinking and feeling? Will you be exhausted? Will you feel defeated? Then, how will you show up as a mom?

I want to turn this myth on its head and invite you to stop thinking of taking care of yourself as selfish. It's actually the opposite! In order for you to show up fully for your family, you need to be able to step into your best self, and it's easiest to do that when you are all filled up.

Even if it's just 10 minutes a day of self-care, you'll be able to show up for your family in a more loving, serving way, which is what you want in the first place.

3 - You have to wait for others to celebrate you

Mother's Day or birthdays are fun days to be celebrated by your family and friends, but I want you to recognize that you don't have to wait for anyone else to celebrate you or wait for a specific date on the calendar.

In fact, I believe you should celebrate yourself every day. Stay focused on all the good things you are doing. Tell yourself you're doing awesome! Despite everything, you keep going and doing what is needed.

There are days when it will be harder to celebrate yourself. Days when you believe you've messed up or said something unkind, but instead of waiting for someone else to show you that you're appreciated, you can accept responsibility for that job.

Understanding the untruth behind these motherhood myths can help you live more peacefully and happily in your purpose as a mom. You've got this!

53

Steering Your Kids in the Right Direction

One of the struggles I hear from my clients is how they can steer their kids in the right direction. You may want to help them get out from under anxious thoughts. Perhaps you want them to return to their faith or stop doing something you disagree with.

There's nothing wrong with wanting your kids to believe what you do or conduct their life in a way you think will bring them happiness. The problem starts when they aren't going in what you define as the "right direction," and you begin assigning meaning to what that means about you and them.

If you define successful parenting as your children following specific behaviors or decisions, you'll find yourself suffering when they don't.

But here's the twist - did you know the definition of successful parenting is totally up for grabs? You get to choose what success looks like for you as a mom.

You are probably carrying around an invisible manual that you believe holds all the rules and definitions of what it means to be a good parent and what your children's actions say about you as a mom.

It's time to look at that manual and ask yourself, "What am I currently thinking makes me a good mom?" Then, question what it means to have your kids on the "right path."

Are you basing your worth on if they are happy, getting good grades, or understanding all that you have taught them? I offer that you might want to avoid going that route. They are not supposed to do all of those things.

They're not meant to be happy all of the time. Sometimes your kids are going to choose not to get good grades. They will decide to step away from what you've taught them. We can do our very best in all these areas, but they may not choose to do any of it.

Because here's the truth - your kids have agency over their own lives. They may choose to make poor choices, or they may go in a way that is 180 degrees from what you had hoped for them.

But, what you do have total control over is your behavior. This is the ONLY thing we have control over when it comes to influencing our kids. You have to show up in your own life and ask yourself whether you are striving to be the best version of yourself. Are you taking ownership and responsibility for how you're showing up? Is this the mom we want to be?

As soon as I try to make my kids do something I think is best for them, I become manipulative. I give my power away to external things, leaving me scared and worried. And when I parent from this place, I'm not showing up how I want to.

What's in your control is what you choose to think and, in turn, believe, which causes how you feel. That feeling will drive your actions and the results of your life. This acceptance allows you to show up for your kids, no matter their decisions, from a place of love and trust.

Renew a Right Spirit within me.
-Psalm 51:10

54

Maximizing Your Role as a Mom

As a mom, we all want to show up as our best selves for our kids, but what if I told you there was a way you could show up 10X more effectively than you are now with just a few mindset shifts?

Here are some areas you can think about and focus on to make small changes toward maximizing your role as a mother.

Understand your worthiness

First and foremost, you need to elevate the relationship you have with yourself. We often talk about "good" and "bad" moms, but instead of trying to label yourself, I want you to recognize your infinite worthiness.

No one and nothing can add to or take away from your worthiness. You are worthy simply because you exist. So, because of that, decide you are a good mom and stop questioning it anymore.

The Truth About Self-Care

Prioritizing taking care of yourself matters! You are filling yourself up as a mom by taking care of yourself. This gives you the energy to show extra love to your family.

Self-care also gives you confidence, allowing you to feel better and go after the things you want for yourself and your family.

Expand your emotional wellness

What would you say your top three emotions are? Are they overwhelm, guilt, worry, confusion, doubt, or frustration? Do you want these to be your top feelings?

We all have exhaustion and to-do lists and the feeling of getting up and doing it all over again, but we don't want to wait to have more joy and balance in our lives. We only get this one life, so we need to start working toward those feelings today. The joyful and peaceful feelings you seek will help you maximize your role as a mom.

Become aware of buffering

Buffering is avoiding uncomfortable feelings by getting a quick dopamine hit with something else. It could be food, alcohol, or social media – anything you're using as an escape. It's important to be aware of when we are buffering because when we do this, we're probably not showing up in the maximum capacity we want.

To be able to maximize your motherhood (and all other areas of your life), we want to expand our ability to handle any uncomfortable feelings and still go forward. When I learned the skill of feeling my feelings, a world of control and steadiness opened up. I was no longer at the effect of my feelings. Expanding this capacity is a great way to maximize your role as a mom.

Be deliberate about enjoying motherhood

I cannot express enough that we have to be purposeful and deliberate about enjoying this journey of motherhood.

There are things that are difficult to find joy in - like being up with a new baby all night or dealing with a difficult teen. However, it's so important to know that whatever stage you're in, don't put off feeling joy. Find what is great about now. Remember, whatever it is - good or bad - is fleeting, and it will pass.

The peace and joy you want as a mom are right here for you - with just a few small tweaks of your thoughts.

55

Having Faith In Your Future Self

As a busy mom trying to balance it all while showing up as my best self, I frequently use this coaching tool to self-coach myself when trying to figure out what I need to do next in my life.

I call it having faith in your future self. It helps us look at where we would love to be in the future and tap into that wisdom to help us decide what next action to take.

First, we want to ask God to guide our thoughts to align with His will. We often forget this step because we're human and get in the groove of life thinking we know what's best for us. But wouldn't we really rather have what God knows is best for us? I simply offer a quick prayer letting him know that I desire his guidance in this process.

Next, we need to take some time to get clear on what we want for our lives down the road. Do you want a different job? Is there a purchase you want to make? Do you envision traveling to specific destinations? Whatever your heart's desire is, focus on the top five outcomes. Write these down somewhere you will see them often.

After you've done that, spend some time visualizing what it would be like to achieve these things in the future. Take one thing at a time and focus on it. What does it feel like? What do you think about yourself? How would you show up? What actions have you implemented to get to where you are? Take your best guess.

Next, imagine yourself sitting across from your future self. What would she tell you? What wisdom would she offer you on how to get from where you are now to where she is? Perhaps she'd say to you that you are worth it. Maybe she'll let you know that, yes, it will get uncomfortable at times, but it's so fun to have it now. Perhaps she'll remind you to slow down and not give up. Don't quit, and all your efforts will pay off. Perhaps she'll tell you it wasn't as hard to achieve as you believe right now.

Whatever it is, you'll learn so much about yourself and what actions to take next.

We are all in different places in our motherhood journey. Some of you seek peace about life with newborns, and some are figuring out your role when your babies are grown up and onto their own lives. Whatever stage you are in, your future self has a lot of wisdom to share about how to live your life right now.

Instead of seeking the answers outside of yourself, you have the option to access your inner wisdom and set in motion what's possible for your life. Having faith in your future self is just one way to do that.

56

A Model That Can Change Your Life

The Model, as we call it in the life coaching world, was created by Brooke Castillo, founder of the Life Coach School, where I was trained. If you've spent any time listening to me or other life coaches, I'm sure you've heard a lot about the model.

The model can be used to identify what you are currently creating for yourself and then help you harness your personal power to decide if that is what you want to keep creating or not. The choice is always yours!

The model breaks everything into five categories (I love simplification!) that show you how everything in your life works together.

The first category is circumstance. Circumstances are the things that happen in the world that we can't control. Circumstances are factual. There is no drama or opinions at all. They are also neutral. Circumstances just exist.

Some examples are how old you are, what you weigh, how many kids you have, what your bank account balance is, or even what your husband said to you this morning.

The next category is thoughts. Thoughts are all the things that happen in our minds. They are the words and phrases that pass through our minds. Thoughts can be challenging to decipher at first, for you've been taught to believe some thoughts are facts.

Some examples are, "I never have enough time," "My children need to behave better," "She shouldn't have been mean to me, and" I can't ever lose weight."

They can be separated from circumstances that are happening outside of you because your thoughts happen inside the mind.

Next is feelings. Feelings or emotions are vibrations that happen in your body. The cause of these feelings is your thoughts, not circumstances. Every feeling you have ever experienced has been caused by you and the thoughts you have chosen to think about your circumstances.

The next category is actions. Our actions are directly related to our feelings. Feelings drive every action or inaction.

This leads us to the fifth and final category, results. The results we have in our lives are the effect of our actions. When you look around at your life and visibly see the things around you, it's all your life results.

The results you create for your life will always be evidence of the original thought, and this is why we look to our minds as our creation power.

As we understand the model, we can create more wanted results and change our internal mental wiring to produce different results.

I love this model so much. It has personally changed my life and helped me create the future I've always dreamed of living. I love how it has the power to change the world one thought at a time.

57

Creating A Peaceful Morning Routine

Have you ever felt that you simply don't have time for a peaceful morning routine? Maybe you don't consider yourself a morning person. Perhaps it just doesn't seem realistic to take the time in the morning to connect to God between making breakfast, getting the kids out the door for school, or getting ready for work and your other responsibilities.

Let me tell you the good news: it is absolutely possible for you to continue your crazy, busy life while effortlessly keeping God as your highest priority.

Can you imagine having plenty of time to connect to Him, the source of all things wonderful, every day because of how you have organized your life?

Prioritizing God is what actually makes life work, and when you prioritize time with him in the morning, you'll find a sense of peace, and even ease will arise so you can handle the rest of the day.

It seems backward to pause, prioritize and make room for prayer when there are so many things pulling for our time and attention. What I know to be true, though, is that when you place God at the center of your life, everything else falls into place. It is the very act of dedicating time to deepen your relationship with God that brings you all your life's desires.

My journey to a peaceful life began with minor, daily tweaks in my priorities. I started by simply setting aside a manageable length of time to pray. I used to see prayer as another item on an already packed to-do list, but committing to this doable amount of time had me looking forward to this time with God.

I also have a spot set aside for this daily practice. I have a small couch that faces a window in my bedroom with a pillow and a comfy blanket. A small side table holds my Bible and other reading materials, along with some candles, rosaries, and a wooden cross. Everything is already gathered for me to use during my daily time or at other spontaneous moments as well.

When you dedicate time to your faith, God will show up for you. He will exponentially bless every part of your life because of the time and attention you are sacrificing for Him. God will note your efforts, even when they aren't perfect, even when they are interrupted.

There are so many ways to make this work for you. Don't get hung up on what you can't do, and focus on how you can make even just a moment in your morning to connect with God. With time, you'll look forward to this time as an essential part of your day.

58

What's Possible For You?

Every single thing that has ever been created by you or by humans, in general, was made from a thought. There are no exceptions to this.

So, if you block yourself from thinking about a particular possibility that you want to create for yourself or don't think purposeful thoughts at all, then you won't create anything in your life on purpose.

Too often, we hold ourselves back from our goals because we allow our brains to go and find all the evidence of things that keep us stuck. This is your brain just doing its job. We have this part of us to keep us safe, comfortable, and energy efficient.

But, when we listen too much to our brain's objections, we fail before we even try.

So, just for kicks, start dreaming - big and small. What small changes do you want for your life?

Do you want to start your own Bible group? Do you want to become a nurse? Do you want your kid's college fund built to a certain number before they go off to school? Do you want to go on regular date nights with your spouse? Lose 20 pounds?

Whatever it is, you must push your brain to places it hasn't gone before. Write down your goals and then brainstorm what it would take to get there and see what you could do today to move forward on those goals.

With that focused attention, you will feel more aligned with the possibility. The way you talk to yourself will shift. Picture what it feels like to have accomplished your goal and start thinking and acting from that place.

You are so capable! And nothing is impossible with God. So after you get it on paper, take it to Him. Ask Him to fortify you with the character traits you need, the courage to get through the uncomfortable parts, and the blessings you need along the path.

You don't have to allow your brain to stop you. Instead, let it be your partner in achieving your dreams. Then, you can have everything you believe is possible in your life.

59

Finding Fulfillment and Living Your Purpose

Maybe you're like me and believe your purpose is something you have to find, discover, go after, or chase. But it's not.

I wanted to know the reason why I existed so I could please God by hurrying up to get there. My brain told me that it had better be good. It had better be noble. And, I needed to be humble about it, so it should probably be something that is of service to humanity.

Intellectually I knew that motherhood was all these things and more. Yet some days, there was still a tugging on my heart that told me I was supposed to be doing something else.

Even reading those words, I know it sounds ridiculous because what could be more purposeful than raising and caring for human beings? But our mind likes to question if we are really living our purpose.

But now, I want to offer you something that may take some time to sink in.

Your purpose is just to exist. Existing is your purpose. The life you are living right now is your purpose.

And here's even better news: since there is no way for you to become more worthy, you just get to choose what to do with your life because you want to, not because you have to, not because you think you should.

You get to choose a purpose that matters to you! And you go about living that purpose because you know you are already good enough.

When it comes to feeling fulfilled, we return to where all the important work is done - your mind.

If you want to feel fulfilled as you carry out whatever it is you are choosing to do, then feeling fulfilled will come from you and nothing outside of you.

You find purpose and create fulfillment for yourself exactly in the place where you are now, in whatever circumstances you find yourself in. It's who you are, and who you get to be. It's something you get to take with you wherever you go.

Choose to believe you are living your purpose and think thoughts that allow you to feel fulfilled.

60

Visualizing Your Dream Life

We all have the God-given ability to take a thought and turn it into a real thing. In fact, to have anything in our future that we don't have right now, we must first think about the new thing.

Yes, only one idea, one vision, one phrase of words put together into a sentence that runs through your brain is the beginning of your creative power.

Once we have the idea of our dream life, then we begin visualizing it - getting all the details, thinking about it, and picturing it. The key is that we have to hold onto that picture. We do that by thinking about it over and over again.

When we become so familiar with the details of our dream life, it begins to feel believable, true, and possible, then it creates strong emotions that compel us to dive into action, and we begin to actually get the things we want and have been visualizing.

Here are 3 steps to help you visualize your dream life:

1 - Picturize

To picturize is to form a picture or vision of what it is that we are wanting. So to begin, answer the question, what do I want?

Sometimes this question can feel too broad, so feel free to break it down into smaller categories. Some examples I use are my home, my business, my relationships, my body, my free time, my spiritual life, and my mental and emotional health.

Once you have your goals, it's time to get into the details. Really picture what it would look like, feel like, and be like to have reached that goal. What kind of feelings do you feel, and what actions do you need to take to make that dream a reality.

2 - Prayerize

After you have decided on your goals for your dream life it's time to take them to God in prayer. You can ask for and follow his guidance, especially by believing in the possibility of what you want and asking for His strength to hold that picture in your thoughts.

Continue having daily conversations with Him about it. What it is that you are after will keep you connected to His divine promptings.

3 - Actualize

Once you have become clear on what you wanted and invoked God's power upon it, you begin taking the actions of realizing your dreams and achieving them. The mental image you created and held on to and then prayed about actually becomes reality.

If you look back on your life and what you have achieved, you will see this is how everything came to you.

Within your mind are all the resources needed to live out what you define as success. The Kingdom of God is within you. It just remains for you to tap into and develop these powers.

61

Celebrating Yourself

In coaching, we talk a lot about how you are 100% responsible for all the results you create in your life. But are you looking around and giving yourself credit for it?

It's also helpful to look back at something you've accomplished and find out how you did it. That way, when your brain tries to tell you that there's something that you can't do, have, or experience, you can say, "Stop right there brain!"

When you celebrate and evaluate your accomplishments, you know exactly what you can do. You know you can create whatever you want!

Too often, we accomplish a goal we set and then immediately move on to the next one. But I'd like to start a revolution of stopping and celebrating more - not only because it feels incredible, but because celebrating itself helps you create better results.

When you're feeling good and enjoying life, you're more likely to take the massive action necessary to continue reaching your goals. You don't procrastinate. It's like this match that's lit, so you keep doing those things that help you feel good.

Our brain is always the first to point out what's not right about the situation, how it wasn't a win, or how you didn't do everything you set out to do. But I want you to tap into your higher brain when celebrating the milestones in your life.

Decide today that you are celebrating all of your accomplishments - relish it. Ask yourself, "How did I do that?" "What was I thinking that allowed me to accomplish this?" "How was I feeling as I worked and reached my goal?"

Don't wait for some later day to celebrate. Instead, look at your life every day and start seeing all the wins that are taking place and celebrate! Everything you want to create in your life is more accessible from that joyful, celebratory place.

62

Curiosity and Courage

It doesn't take much for me to remember a not-so-distant time when I felt overwhelmed, unfulfilled, and behind. I told myself I was smart and should have things figured out by now. I was waiting for motivation to strike me.

When I reflect on where I was then and where I am now, the bridge between these two life stages comes down to two feelings: curiosity and courage. When I took action from these feelings, I began to see the results appear that I had waited and longed for.

Before life coaching, I avoided feeling fear of any kind or doing scary things. I avoided looking at my role in how my life was turning out. I wasn't taking responsibility and instead blamed all the circumstances outside of me.

I didn't want to get to the root cause of my overwhelm, perfectionism, lack of motivation, or lack of fulfillment. After all, it was easier to blame everything else - lack of time, money, other people. I mean, it was their fault, wasn't it? If they would change or do what they were supposed to, I wouldn't have to feel this way. You get the picture.

I wasn't curious or eager to know or learn anything. I was operating in the same old capacity I had come to know and believe was "the path." Take it all on, juggle a million things, work harder, get the degree, do the job, do all the activities, volunteer, make meals, and carve out time for friends. And maybe, I'd eventually get around to taking care of myself once and a while.

I was on a conveyor belt and never stopped to get curious if I wanted ANY of it. I didn't question if I was enjoying it or seeing what was possible for my life.

When I finally slowed down enough to examine my life and got curious about what I could do to improve it, I hired a life coach. She helped me find the path that was best for my life, and that's what I now do for my clients. I can't presume to know what's best for your life. You are the only one who can honestly know.

Curiosity has allowed me to explore all kinds of new perspectives. I've learned a lot of new life skills and a life-transforming way of showing up in the world. And most of all, curiosity has me testing out a bunch of new possibilities for myself.

Here are some of my favorite questions to spark curiosity:

- What do I really want?
- How is this the best thing to happen to me?
- What can I learn here?
- What do I want to try next?
- What would be fun to do if I knew I would succeed?
- I wonder what's possible for me?
- What impact can I make on the lives of others?

Once I got curious, I began to take action to test things out. And this is where I moved to take action from the feeling of courage.

I'll tell you that I still struggle with courage a bit. It doesn't come easy for me, mainly because I spent a lot of my life in perfectionist ways.

But I've learned that playing small isn't the path to living my dreams. Courage is essential because all the effort, work, decision-making, testing, trying, and evaluating will be uncomfortable.

But those actions are the only things that will get you to the point you want.

                    DANIELLE THIENEL

Where in life are you letting your fear win? Where could you be braver? If courage came naturally to you, what would you do?

Give it some thought - how would your life be different if you began to feel curiosity and courage? These feelings are at the root of every success I create in my life these days, and I know it can be for you too.

63

How to Reach Any Goal

Taking action on any goal you set for yourself needs to come from a good feeling. Those good feelings come from the belief that you have about being able to achieve your goals.

As a general rule, every positive result we have created in our life stems from a positive thought, so I welcome you with your goals to choose to think positively about them.

Believe you can reach them. Work to achieve them. All the while thinking positively about your goals and yourself.

This positive momentum will begin to take hold, and you'll find yourself reaching more of your goals.

64

We all want to be more effective moms, wives, and humans. But, when we are under the guise of obligation, overwhelmed, and worried, we can't be as effective in our lives. We are way more effective when we're having fun! Fun allows us to solve our problems, be creative, and invent ourselves anew.

What are some activities that are fun for you? We are created for the pure enjoyment of this human life. Of course, there will be moments of mundane and heavy in motherhood, but there is also so much joy.

You deserve this joy, mama! Deliberately look for ways to add it into your life. Create opportunities through your thoughts and feelings. Direct your mind to experience more fun and joy in your life. Don't wait; find the fun in today.

65

The Pathway to Possibilities

Often the possibility of achieving our dreams feels uncomfortable. You will likely feel uncomfortable, scared, nervous, tired, doubtful, embarrassed, or nervous on the pathway to possibility.

But the good news is those are only feelings! And at the other end is the dream you have been wanting.

In a commercial I once saw, there was the line, "You don't have to be amazing to start, but you have to start to be amazing." That's exactly what I tell my clients about achieving their goals.

To begin, you don't have to have everything lined up ahead of time. You don't have to know every step you're going to take along the way. All that is required is that you start. It starts with taking one tiny step forward, then another, and then another.

The only thing holding you back from taking steps to reach your goals and dreams is your mind. All you are fearing is feelings and vibrations in your body.

Lean into those uncomfortable feelings. They are the currency to reaching all your goals and dreams.

Self Care Isn't Selfish!

I could shout one thing from the rooftops, it would be this: SELF CARE ISN'T SELFISH!

In fact, it's the exact opposite! Self-care is one of the most selfless things you can do. A mom who feels good shows up as her best self.

Stop believing you aren't worth taking the time or spending the money to care for yourself. If you want to be the best person you can be, it's essential.

67

Elevating Your Relationship With Yourself

Before you can begin to change your relationship with yourself, you must first assess where you are. What current beliefs do you have about yourself? Do you want to keep those beliefs, or are you ready to let them go?

Take a sheet of paper and write at the top: What I believe about me is …

Spend some time thinking about that and writing down your thoughts about yourself. For example, do you see yourself as confident? Do you judge yourself a lot, or do you give yourself love and compassion?

Then, you want to evaluate what is keeping you stuck. Perhaps it is perfectionism, fear of failure, or staying stuck in the past. When you identify what keeps you stuck, you can learn to make changes to help you get unstuck and move forward in your relationship with yourself.

Once you understand where you are and where you want to go, it's time to start living in your truth. When you are people-pleasing or worrying about what other people think of you. We have no control and can't change what goes on in other people's minds. No matter what we do or say - even if we believe it's the right thing - it's impossible.

Instead of trying to live based on what other people think, I want to help you come back and live YOUR life, your authentic life. What matters is what you think about yourself. That's all!

You'll elevate your relationship with yourself by learning to have useful thoughts about yourself and your life and living in your truth. And when your relationship with yourself is at its best, you'll find yourself more peaceful, fulfilled, and able to pour into others.

Designing Your Future

In life, we have two choices regarding our future: you can take a back seat and let it unfold, or you can control what you have control over and move toward the future you want.

Think about your life, like your GPS. To get somewhere, you must put in two elements - your current location and the address where you want to go. Just like your GPS, to get to where you want to be in your life, you need to know where you are now and where you're going.

And it needs to be specific. I often tell my clients to get pen and paper and write down their ideal future. Write down as many things that you want that you can think of. And then keep asking yourself, "What else do I want?" "What else sounds fun?"

Once you have a list, the second step is to prioritize and decide what you want to focus on. Pick three to five things. Once you choose what you want to focus on, your brain will start telling you all the reasons you can't achieve it. This isn't a problem. It's just what brains do.

But now it's time to override that part of your brain and deliberately plan how you are going to

overcome the obstacles you've identified in a way that excites, compels, and drives you forward to action.

As you begin to see the future you've pictured and designed taking shape through those small wins, don't forget to celebrate! Even if

    DANIELLE THIENEL

you make a mistake or aren't making much progress, evaluate and learn from those things and celebrate your commitment to making progress on your goals.

You can achieve the future you dream of and have peace of mind along the way.

69

How to Live Your Purpose

If you feel you've lost your purpose, I want you to know that you're not alone. I also want you to know that your purpose is not outside of you. It's not a treasure to be found. It's already a treasure within.

The definition of purpose is the reason something exists. So take a moment to contemplate, what is your purpose?

Your brain will tell you that it doesn't know why you're here and that you better figure it out, or your life will be wasted. It also tells you that it better be something big like helping the planet or the less fortunate.

We look at people we admire, and instead of using them for inspiration, we use them against ourselves to "prove" that we are failing at life.

But, when you stop looking outside of yourself and go within, you can ask and answer the question for yourself.

You don't have to do anything to fulfill your purpose in life. God created you. You exist. So that purpose has already been fulfilled. You are already purposeful! For however long you've been alive on this earth, you have been living out your purpose. Being alive is enough. You don't have to do better.

But once you understand that, now what? What do you do now?

Now instead of stressing about finding your purpose, you get to decide what you will do with your time. What will make your experience while on earth more fun and meaningful to you?

You get to decide right now what you want to do. Is there something out there you want to go and grab? Choose to do that. What stage of life are you in? Choose to be present and purposeful in that.

And whatever you choose doesn't have to be something that stays your purpose forever and ever. It's just where you are right now. So what do you want it to be today?

When you start living in that, you will create, you will contribute, and you will evolve.

So no matter your job or life circumstances, you get to be the person who fulfills your purpose. You get to be that person all the time. And then, by being that person, you'll know what to do next because the doing comes from the being.

In this earthly life, we can't escape the hard parts of it, and our purpose isn't going to be rainbows and daisies all the time, but it's worth it to bring yourself back to the purpose you have chosen for yourself because that is when you are the truest to yourself.

Productivity and Organization

Open your works to the Lord, and your
intentions will be set in order.
-Proverbs 16:3

70

Six Steps To Organize Your Mind

One of the best skills I've learned to create peace for myself is how to organize my mind. Just like physical clutter needs to be sorted, purged, and reorganized, a cluttered mind needs regular attention and care.

Here are six steps to organize your mind:

Step one: Become aware of your thinking with a thought download.

As each thought comes to your mind, write it down and observe it without judgment. Then, just like you'd empty a junk drawer, unpack all the thoughts in your mind by getting them down on paper.

Step two: Examine each thought closely.

Take one thought at a time and observe and evaluate if it is something you still want to keep. It can be helpful to ask questions such as:

- Is this thought serving me?
- Do I really want this thought?
- Is this a current or outdated thought?

Step three: Let go of the thoughts that are no longer useful.

You'll want to overthink this process, but it can be straightforward if you practice. Just as you wouldn't choose to pick up and put on a sweater that doesn't fit, you can choose to no longer think or believe a thought that isn't serving you.

Step four: Determine which thoughts will help you create what you want and upload them.

Instead of a thought download, you'll want to upload new, helpful thoughts. Think of new thoughts you'd like to believe and write them down. It can be beneficial to post them somewhere you will see them often so you can practice thinking about them.

Step five: Ask God for help

God provides the ultimate path to a peaceful mind, and he can guide you to new, higher ways to use your powerful thoughts.

Step six: Be kind to yourself

As you begin this process of organizing your mind each day, be sure to create a space of love and compassion for yourself. Be kind by speaking more gently about yourself and ease up on any judgment that arises.

Trust that the Lord has you in the palm of his hands, and remain curious about the possibilities of creating an organized and peaceful mind each day.

71

The Truth About Balance

Balance is something we are always seeking. We believe we'll feel good when the house is clean, and the kids are doing well in school. Or maybe it's when work is stress-free, and you're able to manage your finances. Perhaps you think you'll find balance when the house is paid off, a vacation is planned, you have the perfect amount of money saved, or the dishes are all put away.

But these are all circumstances you are choosing to view as the reason you're out of balance.

I want to offer to you that balance will never be achieved by looking outside of yourself.

We are constantly growing, expanding, wanting, and needing more and more. We will never be fully satisfied in this lifetime.

Instead, I would like you to focus on your emotions. They are what give you the power to be in or out of feeling balanced. Picture an old-fashioned scale where you put varying objects on each pan and see it teeter-totter back and forth. You add or subtract each side to balance it out. This whole human experience is like that.

We think our lives should remain in balance but what really happens is we teeter back and forth between the 50 percent positive and 50 percent negative in this life. That is actually the goal!

There is supposed to be contrast. You arc supposed to feel off at times. We can't know happiness if we don't understand sadness. We

                                    DANIELLE THIENEL

can't know organization if we don't know chaos. We must meet with defeat to feel success.

Negative emotion doesn't mean something has gone wrong, but our brains, unsupervised, will create more negative emotions than necessary.

Instead, let's embrace that to be a balanced human being, a balanced mom means our emotional experiences will be up and down. Sometimes we will feel like we have it all together, and sometimes, we will feel out of control.

A well-balanced life includes being able to feel negative emotion as if it is part of your life for a great purpose and stop resisting them. You will find freedom, strength, and peace of mind when you choose not to want the things in your life that currently have you resisting, reacting, and avoiding feeling negative emotions and instead accepting all feelings as part of a balanced life.

72

How To Take Back Your Power

Here is something I'm very passionate about: it is never your outside circumstances that cause you to feel a certain way. Never.

It's not about how much money you have, how healthy or unhealthy you are, how many children you have, what your mother-in-law has said to you, how your boss treats you, or how your children behave.

These are all circumstances!

I acknowledge that there are plenty of life circumstances where you might choose to feel sad, disappointed, mad, or frustrated. These are all viable choices. However, the self-pity, guilt, shame, overwhelm, and confusion that come from blaming your outside circumstances will rob you of all your power.

Your power is entirely in what you choose to think about your circumstances.

No one can control what you decide to think about things except you. Once you understand that how you feel isn't something you can blame on someone or something outside of yourself, it is such a relief!

There is no victimhood, self-pity, or blame to be had. Only a renewed power, a new understanding, a new control, and a new responsibility is all yours!

Whatever feeling you want to feel is available to you right now, no matter what is going on around you. Peace is always available to you if you choose peaceful thoughts. Joy is right there when you choose to think joyful thoughts.

The power is yours, and no one can take it from you. Take control of your thoughts and start living the life you dream of.

73

How To Never Have Clutter Again

When deciding whether or not to keep an item in your home, ask yourself the following questions:

1 - Is it serving me?

Is it helping you in some way? Is it something you have used in the last year? Is it something that makes your life better?

2 - Do I really want it?

Was it something that was given to you that you feel like you have to keep? Is it something you bought but now don't enjoy anymore? Do you really want it to take up space in your home?

3 - Is it current or outdated?

Does it fit? Is it broken or damaged? Does it no longer fit into your life?

If you answer no to any of these three questions, it's time to let that item go. Sometimes it can take strength to override your mind saying, "Oh, I might need it," or "So-and-so gave it to me," but if you want a life with less clutter, then you'll need to say goodbye.

Letting go of things that no longer serve you is the key to reducing clutter and creating an environment you love to be in.

74

Three Ways To Make Peaceful Decisions

According to Google, the average person makes 35,000 choices per day. That breaks down to roughly 2,000 decisions per hour when you take out seven hours of decision-free sleep.

It can be little things like what time to get up, what to wear, what to eat, what to do first, how many cups of coffee to drink, or big things like where to live, what career to pursue, or how much money to save.

There is so much power in having a solid decision-making skill set, and because of that, the opposite is true - indecision feels powerless. It is full of confusion, doubt, and worry.

So, here are three truths about decision-making to help you make more powerful and peaceful choices:

1 - The answers are always found inside of you

Whether it's a big or small decision, the answer is always found inside you. But instead of going internally first, we've conditioned our minds to believe that we don't know, and then we immediately go outside of ourselves to look for the answer. But, this just adds more confusion.

Instead of telling yourself you don't know the answer, ask yourself, what if I took my best guess right now? What would the answer be? You want to consciously make decisions for yourself with the power of trust in yourself behind you.

2 - There are no right or wrong decisions

I often find my clients stuck because they fear making the wrong decision. I'm here to tell you there is no such thing. We've been conditioned to believe there is something outside of us that determines whether something is right or wrong for us, but that simply is not the case.

You and I get to decide what is right or wrong by what we choose to think. Even when it comes to your faith and what you believe are absolute truths about right and wrong, it all boils down to thoughts you've chosen to think over and over - so much so that it becomes automatic.

You will grow and evolve and purposefully be in the position of leading your life outcomes when you, on an ongoing basis, keep re-deciding what's right and wrong for you. What you decided once was right in your life may not work for you now. Staying with these outdated beliefs keeps you stuck.

3 - Peace only comes after you make a decision

Once you make a decision, you are in total control of what you choose to think about your decision. You can choose to believe it was the perfect choice for you. Direct your mind to look at how it's working out in your life and why it was the best choice.

When you decisively take action, your next step reveals itself. And you get to keep deciding if you want to keep taking that action or make a change. And, if you are having trouble thinking peaceful thoughts about your decision, you get to decide if you want to make another decision.

Peace comes when you keep moving forward, taking that next right step, and trusting that you know exactly what is best for you.

75

How Not To Be Stuck

Have you ever thought to yourself, or even said out loud, "I feel stuck?" This is something that comes up a lot for the women I'm coaching.

But here's what I want you to know: "I feel stuck" is a thought. You are never really stuck! And the great news is that it's such an opportunity for you to stop and get curious and ask yourself some questions.

Often what we mean by feeling stuck is that we feel that we're not making any forward movement. We're not taking any action that is getting you closer to your dreams. And it's just a new decision we have to make.

Decisions are everything! All the little decisions you're making in your life have gotten you to where you are now and making even more decisions more quickly, more decisively, with strength, with conviction, knowing that you have it inside of you to know what the next step is is what propels you forward.

And it's only in taking action that we get the results we're looking for.

76

How To Turn Confusion
Into Knowing

This tip will seem simple but stay with me. I promise it will give you amazing results.

When you hear yourself thinking the phrase, "I don't know," turn that into a question. Ask yourself, "What if I did know?"

When you do that, your brain will go to work on your behalf, searching to find the answer.

Instead of closing yourself off and feeling confused, you get empowered and take action with forwarding energy.

You'll be able to move forward on your best guess, and you'll find out if that was the right answer or if you need to go back and pick something else.

You will feel immediate relief because confusion is not useful when what we are after is peace.

The peace we want is created in our minds, and asking the question, "What if I did know?" will help you get back to that place more quickly.

77

Action and Inaction

All our actions are driven by feelings, and our thoughts create all our feelings.

It's important to understand that you aren't taking action on something you might want because you haven't created the feeling you need to drive that action.

It's common to expect feelings to just happen to you. Motivation is a great example. So often, we say we didn't exercise because we didn't feel motivated to do it. But motivation is a feeling, and that's something that we can create for ourselves with our thoughts.

Once you understand and take ownership that you are responsible for your thoughts and actions, it's time to do some internal reflection.

What are you doing in your life? How are you showing up? Is it creating the results you want? Do you find yourself not doing the things you want to do?

Then, how do you need to think and feel to drive those actions?

When you become aware of your actions and inactions, you can decide if your actions are giving you the results you want. And if they aren't, no need to be discouraged!

You have all the power you need to change your life in your thoughts.

78

Creating Your Life's Results

Here is something pretty amazing: the only reason you don't currently have the results you want in life is that you don't yet believe the thought that's required to create that result.

This is why knowing your thoughts is so important because they create your feelings, which drive your actions which produce results. It's a bit of a puzzle.

Because I know this, I no longer blame things on anything outside of me. I go within. I capture my power.

This is part of the way our beautiful God created our brains. The answer to changing what you do not like about the human experience and the power to transform what your future looks like is never about changing your circumstances but the way you think about them.

It's not our feelings but our thoughts that create our feelings that result in actions or behavior. Our thoughts directly produce the results we experience in our lives!

Our power always lies in what we are thinking! It does take practice. Sometimes we don't catch it before it happens. Sometimes we don't realize what we're thinking and feeling when life unfolds. But we then go back and evaluate and change what we don't like. It's all progress.

There was a time in my life when I didn't know or understand this yet. But now that I do, I have been able to look at the results I create

     DANIELLE THIENEL

and see my power. As a result, I have more positive beliefs. I take better action.

That is what I want for you too. You are so capable! I know this can change everything for you too.

79

An Answer to Work-Life Balance

I used to love the idea of having a well-balanced life and used to pride myself on doing a great job balancing it all. However, life coaching gives me a whole new perspective on what it means to be a balanced person.

When it comes to balance, the key is to be in the present moment. I find a breakdown often happens when you're in one place, but you have thoughts and feelings that you should be doing something else. Whatever you're currently doing is what you're meant to be doing simply because it is what you're doing.

The truth is that you control how you feel and what you choose to think about it. At the heart of it, work-life balance is simply deliberately and intentionally thinking, feeling, and taking action from what is happening at your present moment, wherever you are.

I'm not saying this is easy. It's a skill that needs to be practiced. But, I believe that if you keep redirecting yourself back to your present moment - living in what is really happening in front of you - you'll feel more in balance more of the time.

How To Stop Procrastinating

Time is our most important asset. We think it's money, but the money goes, and you can get more.

With time, when it's over, it's over. You don't get more. You don't get yesterday back. It's precious. It's fleeting.

How you spend your time is important. And one of the most crucial habits we need to change in using our time the way we want is procrastination.

When it comes to procrastination, I want you to know, first and foremost, that there is nothing wrong with you. The number one thing that we need to do is take more responsibility for managing our emotions.

The more you manage your mind and your emotions, the more you'll recognize that you are the one creating your emotions, and the less you'll use them as an excuse not to go out and do the thing you want to do.

Another reason you may find yourself procrastinating is perfectionism. When I was a perfectionist, I used to procrastinate a lot! I was scared of failing. I was afraid of what other people would think. I was scared of not being perfect. I stayed small.

So, what's the solution?

I'm a big believer in the concept of B- work. You could be doing things today, but you're stopping yourself because you believe it needs to be perfect.

What if, instead of reaching for an A grade, you performed well enough for a B-? This is truly the key to getting started. When something is "good enough," it means you've created something! You've moved toward your goal instead of procrastinating. Done is better than perfect!

81

I Want to vs. I Have to

How often do you say things like:

"I have to cook dinner every day."

"I have to get my child to soccer practice."

"I have to pay this bill by the first of the month."

"I have to lose 10 pounds."

Did you know none of these are facts? They're all just our brains thinking by default. The phrase "I have to" and whatever comes after it implies that it is a must. It's a certainty, a sense of pressure. You are confined or locked in, and the consequences for not doing it would be heavy, devastating, or detrimental to your life.

But there is an alternative to this way of thinking. You can re-word all these, from "I have to's" to "I want to's."

This other way of doing things tells us that deep down if given the absolute choice of doing or not doing something, you would most likely feel that you want to do a lot of the things you are doing.

Take cooking dinner as an example. Instead of thinking that you have to, look for all the reasons why you want to. Maybe you want to nourish your family with healthy foods or pass on your love of cooking. Perhaps you want to give your family the chance to sit around the table and talk over a meal they love.

But, really examine your reasons. Is it true that your kids won't be healthy if they don't have a home-cooked meal every night? Perhaps there are other ways for them to be healthy. Or do you cook a meal every night because you believe that's what a "good" mom does? The truth is, you're a much more effective mom when you are doing whatever makes you feel your best.

Take ownership that no one can make you do anything. You have the power to add or subtract from your to-do list. Even the things our brains try to convince us are mandatory, like laundry or paying taxes, are choices.

You choose it all!

When you feel overwhelmed, resentful, or just busy all the time, bring yourself back to this "I want to" mindset. It's 100 percent up to you and believing this will be a game changer for how you approach your life.

82

Making Your Week Fruitful

As a mom, you're probably familiar with a long to-do list. But there is a way to get everything done that matters without feeling overwhelmed. I like to approach my to-do list by using the five P's.

1 - Prioritize

When you find your mind swirling with all the things you must do, stop and do a thought download, get everything out of your mind, and down on paper. Once it's all written down, take the time to thoughtfully prioritize what matters most to you to get done this week and let go of what doesn't need to be done.

2 - Plan

Take the items you've prioritized and make a plan to get them done. Write them on your calendar or put reminders on your phone. But here's a little trick I used to help myself generate the feelings I need to take action. I put them on my list or my calendar as if they were already done.

So, for example, if I need to buy my kids shoes, I instead write "School shoes purchased." Or, if I want to clean the bathroom, I write, "Bathroom cleaned." This little tweak has made my productivity soar because my brain is going to the place where it's already completed.

3 - Pick non-negotiables

Once you have your plan, pick a few things you are committed to completing this week. Then, commit to seeing a couple of things all the way through from start to finish, and if you get more done, even better.

4 - Pause

Stop to see what thoughts your brain is offering you. When you make a plan, your brain will automatically start doing its job of telling you to seek pleasure and avoid pain. But, if you pause and notice what your brain is doing, you will be empowered to use your higher brain to act intentionally and make progress on your plan.

5 - Payment

When you choose to do something, you'll always be paying for it somehow, typically with your time and effort. Doing what we want to do sometimes means we will have to feel uncomfortable emotions. You may have to feel vulnerable, frustrated, sad, or exhausted.

But afterward, if you hand over that payment, what's on the other side is usually worth it. You will feel pride and success. You will be the person who completes what they set their mind to.

Using these five Ps will increase your productivity and change how you feel about your to-do list.

83 100% Guaranteed

If you knew that your success was 100% guaranteed, what would you go after? What actions would you take? What would that change about your life?

I want you to know that believing you will undoubtedly succeed is a viable option.

  DANIELLE THIENEL

The saying goes, "The only thing certain is death and taxes." And that's true. But even with the certainty of death, that doesn't keep us from living our lives. We go about growing, learning, having adventures, and experiencing things. Instead of fighting it, we step into it.

You can choose to do the same with your goals.

Shift your perspective about going after something. Failing doesn't have to be a problem! Failing can be no big deal. It's the greatest learning tool.

Avoiding negative feelings isn't a good enough reason for you not to go after something you want. And, when you refuse to give up when you refuse to let your fear get the best of you, it is actually 100% guaranteed that you will eventually reach your goal.

Just try this thought with the small things and see how this shift in your mind helps you be the hero of your story and guarantee that you reach all your goals.

84

Circumstance Swapping

One of the most important things you can do to gain control over your mind is to learn to separate circumstances from thoughts about the circumstances. When we overlap thoughts and circumstances, it's challenging to get clarity.

A lot of times in life, when we don't like how we are feeling, we try to swap our circumstances for something else. If you don't like your job, you get another job. If you don't like where you live, you move.

The only problem is when we get to our new circumstances, we still have the same human brain with us, and so we often find ourselves repeating old thought patterns.

I want to challenge you that if you believe that the circumstances of your life aren't making you feel great, first determine what is a fact and what is a thought. Instead of rushing to change your circumstances, take a look at what your thoughts are. See if there is work that you can do there to think about your circumstances in a way that serves you better.

If you can separate the factual information about your life from the story, drama, and thoughts you have about it, then you get to decide, do you want to swap your circumstances, or do you first want to try this power you have? Do you want to look at things differently?

When you choose to think about one circumstance differently, it will change how you look at everything, which is a beautiful thing. If you decide to change your circumstances, you'll be doing it from an empowered place.

85

Already Capable and Set Up

I want to offer you the same encouragement my coach once gave me: you are already capable and set up to make your dreams happen.

Whatever it is in your heart that you want to do, whatever is on your to-do list, whatever goal you want to achieve, you already have everything you need to get it done.

You're so capable. You have gotten to this place in your life. You've already created so many amazing things. Whatever you want to do now is no different.

When you believe you are capable and celebrate where you have already made progress in your life, you'll see that you have everything you need inside of you.

You're capable and set up to reach your dreams. Every day, put your mind there. Don't listen to the part of your mind that wants you to doubt. Instead, use your mind to co-create your life with God. Go after living the life you want.

True Productivity

Are you getting things done? Are you achieving your goals and seeing the outcomes that you want? Are you being productive in your life?

There is a difference between true and false productivity, and it's important to recognize the difference.

First, you have to know what type of action you're taking. There are two types - massive and passive action. We often take action that we think is productive, but it's a passive action. Passive action usually involves learning about something. It's fun for the brain, but if you're not careful, you can get stuck here and never make any progress.

Massive action is the opposite of passive action. It is creating something that will give you results. To take massive action, you must watch your thoughts, especially if what you're after is challenging and you're unsure how to get there.

The second aspect of true productivity is understanding what feelings you are having that are driving your actions. If you are coming from a negative emotion like pressure and dread, it won't necessarily stop you from taking action. You can take action and feel bad at the same time. But I want you to know that it hinders getting your desired results.

You want to take action from feelings that will be self-serving for you. However, when you take action from feelings like committed,

DANIELLE THIENEL

focused, determined, excited, or calm, your productivity will be exponential.

When you learn to stay committed to taking massive action from feelings that help move you forward, you'll find yourself genuinely productive. You'll reach your goals and create the life you want to live.

87

The most important skill you can master when conquering clutter is to let yourself make decisions quickly and confidently.

I love home organizing, and when I used to help people with it when it came to getting rid of things, they frequently hesitated and wondered if they would need that thing in the future, even if it wasn't serving them now. They kept themselves from getting a clutter-free home because they delayed making a decision.

Maybe you've looked at something in your home and decided it's too much work to determine what to do with it right now. Be aware that you're just delaying having to go through the discomfort of deciding in the future when you come across the item again.

Make it a goal to see how quickly you can decide if the items in your home should stay.

Once you get the item out, you get to consciously decide what you want now.

Maybe you'll find something to add to a shelf that makes you smile, find the perfect way to organize your drawer now that you have more space, or find an item to add to your wardrobe that you didn't realize you were missing.

When you say goodbye to what's no longer serving you and let it go, you have the space to focus on your future.

This is how we conquer clutter and free up space in our minds.

5 Ways to Achieve Balance

1 - Define what balance is for you

Brains love specifics, and so to achieve balance, you need to know what it means to you. Ask yourself, "What does my life look like when it's balanced?" Then, "What does my life look like when it's out of balance?"

Are you yelling at your kids? Rushing around and feeling behind? Do you feel like you don't have enough time and too much to do? These kinds of things can be hints that something isn't right.

Think about times when your life has felt in balance. What were some things you were doing, thinking, and feeling? Reflecting on these times can help you define what balance means for you.

2 - Define what your role as a mom is in your current stage of motherhood

Balance looks different in every stage of motherhood. Whether you are a mom of toddlers, teenagers, or kids who are grown, your role and the level of hands-on involvement in your kids' lives will look different.

Once you're clear on where you are in your motherhood journey, define what balance would realistically look like during this stage of motherhood.

3 - Define how you want to spend your time

It's so important to understand how you are spending your time and if you like the way you are spending it.

If the way you spend your time doesn't align with your priorities in this season of your life and motherhood, then you get to re-decide to spend it in the way that keeps you and your life in balance.

4 - Define your future

What goals do you have for your future, and how on track are you to reach them? When you put some time and attention into this question, you will become more balanced because you know where you're going and making progress toward that.

When you know where you're headed, there's not much questioning when thinking about taking on something new. You can always ask, "Does this fit into my ultimate plan for my future?"

We can't feel balanced in our lives if we don't know where we're going. And so we want to really define goals so that we're not distracted from where we want to be.

5 - Call on your faith

As a member of the Catholic Church, I draw on our sacraments and the church's teachings to guide me. Whatever your faith, when you connect to our Creator in some fashion, you can use that relationship to create a more balanced life.

Draw on your beliefs to help and guide you on your next steps. I am always telling my clients not to hurry. That a mom who feels balanced isn't in a rush, she has an unhurried spirit about her. I equate that with God's rhythm. God doesn't rush. He is steady and calm, and He always encourages.

You are never alone. I love enhancing my life by calling on my faith to help me regain balance because I know I am never alone with His help.

 DANIELLE THIENEL

Trust in the Lord with all your heart, and
do not lean on your own understanding. In
all your ways acknowledge Him, and He
will make your paths straight.
-Proverbs 3:5-6

89

Motherhood can feel like a lonely journey, but you are not alone! We mess up. We do things we never thought we would do. We fall short.

As mothers, we are all going through the same struggles, and it is in the openness of communicating with others that you learn you are not alone.

While we may feel lonely at times, that feeling is never caused by circumstances outside of us. Instead, it is caused by the way that we think about the things happening around us. This is such great news!

You get to choose to believe that you are going through the exact same trials as other moms and that you can reach out and talk about them. Or you can choose to simply believe that what you're feeling is normal and that you're not alone.

You can also choose to believe that God is with you always. Picture Him beside you now. Picture Him walking and talking with you. Picture yourself in his embrace. You can always turn to Him in your moments of loneliness and speak to Him about all your troubles as plainly as you would to a friend.

You are not alone, momma.

90

Seeking God's Rhythm

There is no doubt that we are a culture of busyness, and it's hard not to believe that we have to run from morning to night just to keep up. But, when you're jumping non-stop from one activity to the next, you'll miss where God resides - in the quiet, in the silence. He is never rushed and always peaceful.

God doesn't keep up with us. He is waiting for us to seek Him. If you go at one pace while God is going at another, you will always be out of sync. It is time to step off the merry-go-round and become attuned to God's rhythm.

To do this, you have to be deliberate and carve out breaks from the noise of life. If you make that effort, God will meet you right there with your good intentions.

And, while you lean into an unhurried pace, the Lord will help you find all the right responses to your difficulties.

The more peaceful you are, the more God acts now.

Feeling Christ's Peace

When we are faced with difficult circumstances, there are endless ways to think about the situation in ways that create different feelings. What you choose to think creates an emotion that is totally optional. You get to decide.

However, our brains are still human with faults and frailties. Because of this, each morning, before I get out of bed, I ask God to direct my thoughts to Him and fill me with patterns of thinking that are closer to His way.

We won't be able to constantly sustain a feeling of peace always while living on this Earth. It's not what the human experience was meant for. Instead, we are supposed to feel an array of feelings and have a variety of experiences to fulfill our Earthly purpose.

But, the path to more lasting peace is a grace given to us through Christ alone. He is here to be our partner in changing our thoughts and lives to experience more peace.

You don't have to do it alone.

92

Goal Setting With God

Goal setting is a spiritual practice. It's a very compassionate and wonderful thing to do for ourselves because allowing ourselves to dream helps fulfill God's desires for us. God wants us to be aware of our heart's desires and take action to go after achieving them. He also wants us to call on Him as we reach for our goals and enjoy our time on Earth.

If you're feeling unfocused, don't have a clue of what your heart's desire is, or feel like you're wandering haphazardly through life, I invite you to consider setting some goals that will move you forward to joy, challenge you to show yourself what you are capable of creating, and build strength in your muscles of faith.

Once you declare your goals, your mind will offer you all kinds of reasons why you can't achieve these goals. This isn't a problem at all. In fact, it is exactly what a normal human brain does to try to protect you from doing hard things.

So what you need now is a plan to overcome. This is the time to go to God because He is the ultimate conqueror. This is where God wants us to learn to stop trying to control everything ourselves and instead look to Him for help.

I like to pray to get more clarity on what is worthy of my time and attention as I reach for my goals. I ask the Lord for His wisdom and invite Him to take control of my results because He knows my future and what's best for me.

Dream big. Meet and overcome obstacles. Enjoy the journey and evolve into the best version of yourself.

93

Grace and Gratitude

There is nothing more life-changing than gratitude. Gratitude opens up a space of light in every experience we have. Nurturing gratitude for our current lives will awaken the grace that is already residing inside us. It opens up a path for grace to flow.

Grace is the love and mercy given to us by God. He freely gives it, and every one of us already has the grace of God within us. Everything about our life is by the grace of God. The easiest and most laser-focused way for you to access the grace of God is through gratitude.

Picture a hectic morning of trying to get everyone up, ready for school, and out the door. One mom may only see the chaos of it all, wishing everyone was doing more and getting themselves ready. That mom will show up frustrated and critical.

Another mom may choose to look at the hustle and bustle of a crazy morning as a blessing of time with her wonderful family, who are each doing their own thing and getting ready at their own pace. Maybe she enjoys time with one of her children, brushing and braiding their hair and talking about what dreams they had the night before. She is focused on how grateful she is to have these children, home, and life and shows up from a place of joy and peace.

You can choose to cultivate gratitude by how you think about things. When you are aware of how perfectly you fit into creation and how abundant your life is, grace changes your perception. Your thinking is raised higher and focuses on the positive.

DANIELLE THIENEL

Gratitude changes your relationship with life from reacting, avoiding, and resisting things, to viewing what is happening around you with acceptance and appreciation for what is.

You activate gratitude by giving it your attention and must direct your mind there on purpose. It will create a whole new energy flow for you. You'll show up more as your true self, and everything within you and around you will change.

Whenever you think thoughts that bring on the feeling of gratitude, it builds a neural pathway in your brain. The more you do it, the deeper the pathway gets, like a well-walked hiking trail. These new pathways change your perception and allow you to pay attention to the good things in your life more and more.

When your mind is occupied with gratitude, you have no time for worry or complaints. As a result, negative thought patterns lose their strength. They grow weaker and weaker, and a grateful heart emerges, bringing you peace and joy.

94

Do you ever find yourself feeling defeated like you just can't win, or that the cards are stacked against you? Do you feel like you've tried and tried again, but you're getting nowhere?

But feeling defeated is just that - a feeling. And all of our feelings come from our thoughts. You don't have to stay feeling this way.

Because our mind is so powerful, we sometimes need a tool to help us overcome these thoughts. To beat defeat, we have to focus on the opposite. We have to focus on what strengthens us.

Here are three powerful Bible verses that I have found very helpful in overcoming defeat. When you choose to think these thoughts instead of the ones that bring you to defeat, you'll find yourself feeling stronger.

Philippians 4:13

"I can do all things through Christ who strengthens me."

This is one of my all-time favorite Bible verses! Christ is all-powerful. He wants the best for us. God created us, and when we think about Him by our side, giving us the strength we need, it gives us a surge of belief.

Romans 8:31

"If God is for us, who can be against us?:

I love to picture myself lined up against all my obstacles. But the best part is, I'm not alone. God is standing beside me. Because He's on my side, and there's nothing greater than Him, how could I lose at anything I tried to accomplish or overcome?

Mark 9:24

"I believe; help my unbelief."

This verse reinforces two things: our faith and our humanness. You have enough faith to be calling on the divine, but you are doing it from a vulnerable place. Every time I think the thought, "I believe; help my unbelief," I feel a surge of power to overcome my negative thoughts.

I encourage you to try these verses when you feel defeated when you have obstacles in front of you, or whenever you think you've tried and don't have the gumption to try again. Redirecting your mind to these verses can help you create more peace in your life.

95

Faithful From The Inside Out

When my clients come to me, they usually bring an external problem. It could be something like their business isn't making money, they don't know how to get a handle on their anger or frustration, they can't stop eating cookies and candy, or any other outside circumstance.

But, as a coach, I know that what first needs to change comes from the inside.

To make these internal changes, you have to have faith in yourself. Faith in yourself comes from the inner life you build around yourself, and it's imperative you have your own back, especially when you mess up!

So how much faith do you have in yourself? Faith is a firm persuasion, an assurance, a conviction. Faith is confidence in what we hope for and an assurance that the Lord is working in our lives, even if we can't see it.

You will begin to see the results of your life sprout when you order your internal thoughts.

Putting the negative parts of your past behind you is a great place to start! From there, you can purposefully begin to have a deep conviction that you are capable, strong, and deserving of the change you want to see.

Faith in ourselves doesn't rely on what we have racked up in our past as evidence, and that evidence has no bearing on what your future will be. It's up to you; what you're thinking and feeling about yourself directly impacts the future.

Faith allows us each morning to open our eyes to a new day, try again, return to thoughts that make us feel capable, and reach our goals.

It is your right to live an abundant, prosperous, joyous, and peaceful life. You have the power to decide what you will create each day, knowing that God will help you when you ask.

It's not outside evidence that spurs you to be more faithful; it's the inside life you create.

96

God's rhythm is slow, calm, tender, and peaceful. He's not in a hurry. If you want to align your life more with Christ, you'll want to align yourself to his rhythm. Ask yourself, why do I rush? Why do I hurry? What if there is plenty of time?

Whatever you're after, know that you don't need to hurry to get there. Instead, take time to rest by the wayside. A leisurely pace accomplishes more than a hurried one. When you rush, you forget what matters most. You can't draw on your inner wisdom when moving frantically.

And, if you're hurrying somewhere to obtain a specific feeling you'll have when you get there, remember, you can have that feeling now!

You can be calm and unhurried, slow and steady. In fact, that may even get you to where you want to be more quickly, for God's rhythm is the best example.

He never rushes, and everything is good in time. It takes nine months to grow a human, a whole season to grow a harvest, and sometimes it takes years for the goals and desires of your heart to appear.

So, it's time to adopt a new mantra, one that will align you with God's rhythm - easy does it. When you believe that "easy does it," you will remember to enjoy what matters: the journey, not the destination.

A more certain, less hurried way of life is available to you. You don't have to let society tell you to do more and do it faster. Instead, take things in your stride. If you keep moving, regardless of your pace, you'll get there and see the next step you should take more clearly.

Easy does it, mama.

97

What God Can Do For You Today

As part of my morning routine, I take a small notebook and divide it into two sections:

1. Things I am going to do today

2. Things God will do for me today

In the section of things I'm going to do today, I always have a couple of things that are very similar from day to day. Prayer, cleaning, exercise, and visiting my parents. I also add the things scheduled that day, like taking the kids to the orthodontist or the number of clients on my schedule. In the end, I have my list of things that I have control over accomplishing that day.

Here is where all of the grace starts pouring in. There are always items I want to complete but don't have control over. For example, perhaps I'm worried about my parents or kids, and I want God to strengthen them. I write that in the Things God will do for me today column.

I may want Him to help me relax and be more present. I put that in that section. I'm always asking for Him to inspire my thoughts and help guide and inspire my words whenever I work with clients.

I want my family to be healthy. So, in my section, I might put "buy vitamins" or "sign up for flu shots." Those are tangible things I can do. But, it feels much more peaceful for me to hand over my worry about my kids going to school and the fact that they might get sick to God. So I write a note for the protection of my kids today in the list of things God will take care of.

If you don't know what to do, if questions swirl in your head, let God take care of that for you. He will guide your discernment, and you will know it is being taken care of because He says, ask, and you shall receive.

Anytime I write anything down in the section about what God will do for me, I have a sense of peace knowing that I've asked and He will do those things. Even if there's not a tangible result for me to see, I then know His answer was just "Not now," which is so comforting.

We can't do it all, even though we often try. But we could get things done more quickly and calmly if we handed some things over to the One who can take care of it all.

98

My coach and mentor, Jody Moore, teaches this formula:

Acceptance + Grace = Progress

Often, I find that my clients argue about what's going on in their lives and where they are. But, when we argue with reality, we lose our power. You can tell the story of your past, present, and future in the way that best serves you. When you accept where you are, you can work with your life instead of against it.

Grace is the next crucial part of the equation. The spiritual definition of grace is that it is generous, free, totally unexpected, and under deserved. It's an attribute of God that is most manifest in the salvation of sinners.

It's also important to give yourself grace. You are a human with a human brain. You will make mistakes. You will do things wrong. You will fall short. But as moms, we need to stop being our own worst critics and instead show up like a best friend.

Would you talk to your best friend (or even a stranger, for that matter) the way you speak to yourself? Would you say the things to her that you say to yourself when you have a human moment? Or would you offer her grace, understanding, and compassion?

I'm willing to bet you would tell her she was doing her very best and encourage her to keep trying and keep going. Be that friend for yourself.

Tell yourself, "There I go being human again." When you yell at your kids, forget to do something for someone, or get to the end of the day without finishing your to-do list, tell yourself, "There I go being human again."

You can't beat yourself up or hate yourself into showing up better! But when you show yourself love, compassion, and grace, you'll begin to make changes. The grace you give yourself will allow you to progress on the behaviors and actions in your life that you want to change.

I love knowing I'm full of grace. Grace comes from my Heavenly Father but also from the love and compassion I show myself when I don't act from the place of my best self. I wish that for every mama. Start giving yourself more grace than ever, and watch how your life will transform.

<h1 style="text-align:center">99</h1>

Giving Thanks With Appreciation

It's a basic fact that everyone craves appreciation. I hear from many moms I work with that they feel that no one appreciates all they do for their families. So, if you feel like this, I want you to know that you can change it right now.

To experience the feeling of appreciation, you don't have to rely on anything outside of yourself. Appreciation is an emotion and feeling we experience through the thoughts we choose to think.

When I think thoughts like, "I'm a rockstar mom," "I take great care of my family," or "I follow through on what I say I'm going to do," I feel appreciation for myself.

What can you think about yourself that you did in the past that you can appreciate?

Thank yourself for going to college, for going to the gym regularly, and for not giving up when things got tough.

What are you doing right now that you can thank yourself for?

Are your kids fed? Are they dressed? Did they get bathed? Are they getting a foundation, or are you trying to give them a foundation in faith?

Just off the top of your head, I bet you can think of a whole list of things to thank yourself for. And, when you appreciate yourself, it will be easier to give appreciation to others. When you live life from a place of thankfulness, you can't help but feel good.

100

Connecting Your Faith

My faith is the foundation for everything I do in life. Before I set a goal or make a plan, I call on my faith to bless them. Staying connected to my faith helps me feel on top of things and find more satisfaction in my life.

Calling on your faith can allow you to level up in all areas.

To enhance your faith and connect with it daily, we want to acknowledge that the thoughts in your mind are yours to cultivate. Can you bring your thoughts more toward faith daily?

It takes practice because our mind is easily distracted by the task at hand, but you can learn how to be present faithfully while still functioning in your daily life. I admit that staying conscious of Jesus when I'm busy is challenging. But as much as I can as I go about my life, I try to turn my thoughts to Him.

Another way to connect more deeply to your faith is to look at the pace at which you're living your life. Why do we need to hurry? What's the rush?

When we step into God's rhythm, we are reminded that He is not hurried or rushing. He is calm and peaceful. This thought always calms me when I find myself rushing. There is no rush because His rhythm is best.

Courage is another critical component of faith. Whenever I need to call on courage in my life, I connect with my faith by going to the Lord and being reminded of how often He told us do not be afraid. I picture those words coming into my heart, and it automatically gives me courage.

We worry about many things - children, money, relationships, and whether we're doing a good enough job. This is the perfect time to call on your faith. Recall that He tells you do not be afraid and call on your courage.

You are never alone. Christ is always present with you. You can always call upon Him. Remembering that and connecting to your faith daily will bring you more peace, joy, and every good thing in your life.

Resources

Book a call: https://www.daniellethienel.com/my-calendar-page

Podcast link: https://www.daniellethienel.com/podcasts/the-peaceful-mind-podcast

Website link: https://www.daniellethienel.com/

Blog link: https://www.daniellethienel.com/blog/

Instagram link: https://www.instagram.com/daniellethienelcoaching/

Danielle is a wife, mom of three, member of the Catholic faith, certified life coach, author and host of The Peaceful Mind Podcast for Busy Moms – and she's familiar with the stress and overwhelm busy moms face on a daily basis. She dreamed of being a mom and having a family, but when it finally happened, the reality of the vocation was that it was more challenging than anticipated. Instead of the joy and ease hoped for, days were full of frustration, guilt and hustle and she found herself dreaming of the day she would feel a sense of peace and control… and then found the way!

She now knows that we all have the power to create any result we want for our lives and that this power comes from Christ. Our loving God placed desires for peace, balance, and a better life in our hearts for a purpose, and He gave us our minds to co-create with Him while on Earth.

Danielle's story started when she was working outside the home at a job that didn't align with what she truly wanted. She was in the middle of renovating a house, moving her parents, taking care of kids, driving her kids to all their different extracurricular activities, and not taking care of herself. She thought she could manage everything, but all she really accomplished was managing herself into a sickbed.

She contracted the flu and bronchitis and was forced to be still for two whole weeks. During that time, something she can only describe as "divine" happened. She knew in her soul that she was being divinely guided. She listened to that voice and started making changes in her life that would allow her to be at home, prioritize everything going on, and focus on her faith, family, and herself.

Suddenly, everything started to fall into place. She learned a completely different approach to everything: a process and a blueprint to living life from a place of total control. Life coaching offered a whole new way of doing things in a simpler, sustaining, and empowering way. She became certified as a life coach with The Life Coach School and then studied further, achieving an Advanced Certification in faith-based coaching.

She has since focused her life coaching practice on helping other moms find the joy, balance, and peace she is now an expert in creating. She's dedicated to maximizing her clients' God-given potential and helping moms care for themselves more deeply - mentally, emotionally, and spiritually - so they can have lives filled with more peace, balance, and joy. Within her coaching practice she uses podcasting as a method to get her message out and created this book, The Peaceful Mind Bible to reach those book readers who might not access podcasts. To hear Danielle share the wisdom found in these pages as an extended audio version of each of the 100 treasures you read, you can go to The Peaceful Mind Podcast for Busy Moms on any one of the major podcasting platforms or by visiting daniellethienel.com.

You can also read her first book *The Cyclone Mom Method: How to Call Upon Your God-Given Power to Remain Calm, In-control and Confident as a Busy Mom* by going to: daniellethienel.com.

Danielle believes that we are all born with a gift we were meant to share. Coaching is the vehicle she was given to share her gift. She can show you how to find your path, too.

Any reader, any mom, is also invited to meet Danielle using this link to book a time on her calendar: https://www.daniellethienel.com/my-calendar-page.

Acknowledgments

Heartfelt love and gratitude to the following for the support to make this book possible:

Thank you to The Father, The Son and The Holy Spirit

Thank you to my husband Mark

Thank you to my children and parents

Thank you to Whitney

Thank you to Carrie

Thank you to all my life coaching clients past, present and future- I love you all, I am so proud of you and inspired by you- and it is my greatest honor to be your life coach